TM

so you waɪ̣ ṭ ṭo…

STaRT a

BLOG

A Step-by-Step Guide to Starting a Fun & Profitable Blog

By Rebekah Sack

Foreword by Ray Higdon, founder of the
Ray Higdon Private Blogging Association

SO YOU WANT TO START A BLOG: A STEP-BY-STEP GUIDE TO STARTING A FUN & PROFITABLE BLOG

Copyright © 2016 Atlantic Publishing Group, Inc.
1405 SW 6th Avenue • Ocala, Florida 34471 • Phone 800-814-1132 • Fax 352-622-1875
Website: www.atlantic-pub.com • Email: sales@atlantic-pub.com
SAN Number: 268-1250

Library of Congress Cataloging-in-Publication Data

Names: Sack, Rebekah, 1994- author.
Title: So you want to start a blog : a step-by-step guide to starting a fun &
    profitable blog / by Rebekah Sack.
Description: Ocala, Florida : Atlantic Publishing Group, Inc., [2016] |
    Audience: Age 12-20. | Audience: Grade 9 to 12. | Includes bibliographical
    references and index.
Identifiers: LCCN 2016021971| ISBN 9781620232170 (alk. paper) | ISBN
    1620232170 (alk. paper)
Subjects: LCSH: Blogs--Juvenile literature.
Classification: LCC TK5105.8884 .S23 2016 | DDC 006.7/52--dc23
LC record available at https://lccn.loc.gov/2016021971

Printed in the United States

Printed on Recycled Paper

Reduce. Reuse.
RECYCLE.

A decade ago, Atlantic Publishing signed the Green Press Initiative. These guidelines promote environmentally friendly practices, such as using recycled stock and vegetable-based inks, avoiding waste, choosing energy-efficient resources, and promoting a no-pulping policy. We now use 100-percent recycled stock on all our books. The results: in one year, switching to post-consumer recycled stock saved 24 mature trees, 5,000 gallons of water, the equivalent of the total energy used for one home in a year, and the equivalent of the greenhouse gases from one car driven for a year.

Over the years, we have adopted a number of dogs from rescues and shelters. First there was Bear and after he passed, Ginger and Scout. Now, we have Kira, another rescue. They have brought immense joy and love not just into our lives, but into the lives of all who met them.

We want you to know a portion of the profits of this book will be donated in Bear, Ginger and Scout's memory to local animal shelters, parks, conservation organizations, and other individuals and nonprofit organizations in need of assistance.

*– **Douglas & Sherri Brown**,*
President & Vice-President of Atlantic Publishing

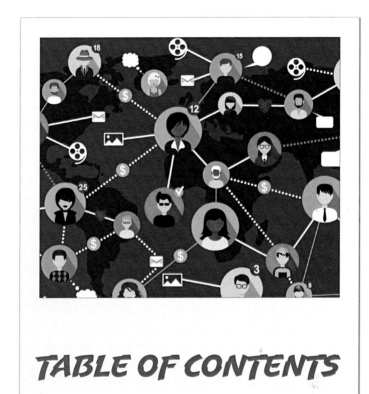

TABLE OF CONTENTS

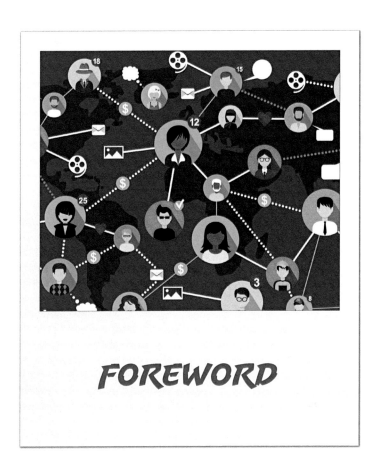

FOREWORD

I was honored to be asked to write the foreword for this book: "So You Want to Start a Blog: A Step-by-Step Guide to Starting a Fun and Profitable Blog." You see, I've been a blogger for six years now and have actually created over 1,800 blog posts. Blogging is my number one online marketing strategy that has helped me go from being dead broke and in personal foreclosure to building a multimillion-dollar a year business from home.

I believe that blogging is not only the best marketing mechanism that exists on the planet, but I also believe it's becoming, if it's not already, the most trusted way to get a message out to the world.

What you have in your hands here is a way for you to build a business from home with very little overhead, very little money output, and just following a few sets of rules that will help you build an audience, perhaps become an authority, and attract the perfect people to you.

I believe that starting a blog is one of the smartest things you can ever do to build an audience, make extra money, and funnel your energy into whatever you are passionate about. There are bloggers for just about every niche or interest nowadays, and this trend will only continue.

The fact that you have this book — it means that you're probably looking for ways to make some extra cash or to spread the word about something you're passionate about. You can make these things happen with a blog. There are some fundamental things that I would suggest to you.

Number one: Understand who you are wanting to attract and what is valuable to them. You can be educational or entertaining, but knowing who you would like to attract to you is critical.

Number two: Be consistent. The people we want to attract to us are home business owners, entrepreneurs, and those wanting to learn online marketing strategies to build their business. We know they hunt for information on a daily basis, so we provide value daily via our blog, our podcast, and other social media avenues.

Number three: Have fun with it! Young people are told all the time to do what makes sense or to go into careers that are in high demand. We say that life is meant to be ENJOYED not ENDURED and to run after something worth catching. Pick something to blog about that you actually like to talk about, and the readers you attract will blow your mind.

Blogging has been the absolute No. 1 marketing key for our business to help us get out of debt, out of foreclosure, out of being dead broke, and to building a massive audience. We now have an email list of over 160,000 people that generates a lot of money, and we have a lot of fun doing it.

Congratulations on picking up this book. I'm sure you'll get some massive value out of it. All I hope for you is that you take action, move forward, and start blogging about the things that you're excited and fired up about. I believe the world needs more fired up, excited people, and I hope that that's you.

– Ray Higdon,
Founder of the Ray Higdon
Private Blogging Association

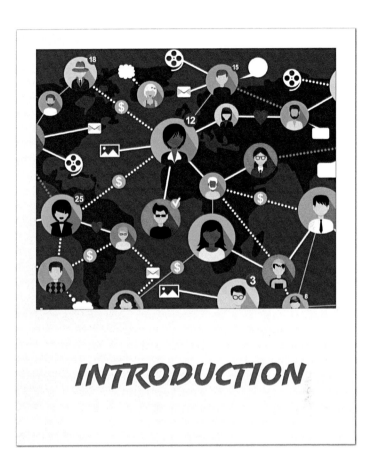

INTRODUCTION

Y ou're here because you want to a start a blog. It can be intimidating when you see what else is out there — how will I ever be as fashion-savvy as Tavi Gevinson? How could I ever be as quirky-cool as Zoella? These teens have taken a passion and have transformed them into… well, into empires.

It might be a mistake to pick up this book and think that you're only a few pages away from becoming the next big Internet sensation (though we're all for dreaming big). What this book can do is give you some guidance when it comes to the daunting world of blogs — the blogosphere, or so it's called.

It doesn't matter what stage you're at, either. You have a blog, but you want to start making money? Flip over to Chapter 6. You want more exposure for your blog? Head on over to Chapter 7. You don't even have a topic picked out yet? That's fine — hit up Chapter 3.

No matter what stage of life your blog is at (barely breathing or on life support), you'll be sure to find some answers between these covers. To keep your short attention span engaged, you can scan the pages easily, because we've made the paragraphs super short.

Scanning has never been such a dream.

Really.

You'll also be glad to know that there are fun facts pretty much everywhere — even if you're a total blog expert, I'm sure you don't know everything.

> ☞ *Fast Fact:*
> Every half a second, a new blog is created.

Okay, maybe you knew that, but we promise that you'll learn something new.

Get ready to learn everything from blogging etiquette to the basics of design, because you're about to crown yourself the master of blogging.

CHAPTER 1
BLOGGING 101

Before you can start designing and creating content for your blog, you need to know what a blog is and how it functions. There are entire books dedicated to the history and understanding of blogging, but we won't make you read through all that.

Get ready for your crash course in everything **blog**.

What is a Blog?

A blog is a combination of the words Web and log. It's a website where you write entries or "postings," and they're usually seen in reverse chronological order.

Blogs can be about any subject — seriously, anything. Here are some popular topics:

- Politics
- Fashion
- World events

- Daily life
- Public opinion
- Food and cooking
- News
- Beauty
- Literature
- Reviews
- ...Anything your heart desires

You'll also see some personal blogs from celebrities, world leaders, and aspiring political candidates. If you can think of a theme, there's going to be a blog related to it.

Top 3 Earning Bloggers in the World [from *The Richest* (2014)]

1. Tech Crunch founder Michael Arrington: $500,000 – $800,000 per month

2. Mashable founder Pete Cashmore: $560,000 – $600,000 per month

3. PerezHilton founder Mario Lavanderia, 'Perez Hilton': $200,000 – $400,000 per month

Personal blogs are often considered online versions of a diary or journal. Although this is a pretty good comparison, blogs are way different than a paper-based diary or journal, since you can do *cool online stuff* with them. (We know that's not very technical language, but you know what we mean.)

A blog uses a combination of text, graphics, images, and hyperlinks to other blogs, websites, Web pages, and multimedia content, such as movies or audio clips.

One of the features connected with blogging are comments — this is where the *cool online stuff* comes in. A blog opens the door to two-way communication between yourself and literally millions of people on the Internet. Be careful, though — you're bound to see at least one super weird comment.

The key difference between a Web page and a blog is that a Web page is static content, which means you can read the page, but you can't really interact with it.

When you start your blog, you will officially be a blogger. Since there are millions of blogs, there are millions of bloggers, and that number grows every day as blogging continues to increase in popularity.

You may just want to start a blog for fun — maybe you envision it as a place where your family and close friends can stay up-to-date with your life. But for those of you who want to go above and beyond and potentially reach thousands (or millions) of people, you're going to learn that successful blogging has a lot to do with promoting it (see Chapter 7).

On websites, links can help raise visibility with search engines. The same is true of blogging. Links to and from blogs to other blogs and websites are directly related to the popularity and overall visibility and ranking of blogs.

The Blog Timeline

1990s: This is when blogging originated. Arguably, blogging has its roots in elementary website functionality, which allowed websites to link (through HTTP hyperlinks) to other sites.

1994: Blogging pioneer Justin Hall launches Justin's Links from the Underground, which is essentially a website for reviews of other websites and a personal online journal in which he posts daily entries and updates for an ever-growing reader base. From these humble beginnings, others copied and modified the format of the blog and launched the blogging revolution.

1997: The term "Weblog" has been coined and is commonplace terminology for Web-savvy people.

2000: Blogs have exploded in popularity, expanding beyond personal journals into the world of business, politics, and nearly every aspect of the World Wide Web.

2016: Over 409 million people view more than 22.6 billion pages each month (figure taken from **https://wordpress.com/activity**).

Throughout this book, you will see the term "blogosphere." The blogosphere is a collective community of all blogs throughout the World Wide Web. Essentially, the blogosphere is the compilation of all blogs, including personal, business, political, or otherwise, on all websites. The blogosphere is not a single, physical place or website; rather, it is a term coined to describe the place where all blogs live, very similar to how we use the term "Web" today.

Keep in mind the dynamic relationship of blogs within the blogosphere. What makes blogs unique is the interaction between the author and the readers. A blog is an ongoing dialogue in written format on Web pages, each a small part of the overall blogosphere.

Why Should I Start Blogging?

Okay, so blogging is kind of cool, but what's in it for me? Turns out there are tons of reasons to start blogging — here are five.

1) Make money

So, this may not be the most important one in mom's eyes, but what's wrong with a little extra cash in your pocket? If you use Google AdSense on your blog, you can start advertising for some pocket money.

It won't be much when you first start out, but there are a lot of teens out there who make more than just some piggy bank change — many teen bloggers make enough money before they graduate high school to help pay for college. Tell that to mom and dad!

2) Improve your skills

One of the best reasons to start a blog is to improve your skills. A lot of employers look to hire people who have a wide list of skillsets, and many look for people with computer and design experience.

It would look pretty awesome if you could put your blog experience on your resume — not only would you be showcasing your writing and editing skills, but you'd be impressing your recruiter with your website design experience.

3) Unleash your creativity

Everyone has the ability to be creative (at least we'd like to think so). Sometimes, it can be hard to find a way to unleash that side of you. Many teens do it through art or music class, but some just don't jive with that kind of thing. If you want to be creative but can't paint or sing to save your life, try blogging.

Not only is the writing part of blogging going to unleash your creativity, but the design part will, too. Creating the layout, choosing the design elements, and selecting photographs and multimedia components to supplement your blog all work to hone in on that creativity you were born to use.

4) Jazz up your routine

We all know how school can sometimes put us in a slump. My day used to look like this: Wake up and get ready. Go to school. Come home. Sit on the couch and watch TV (occasionally play a computer game like SimCity), eat dinner, and go to bed.

I felt like I was wasting my time. Some of my friends went to dance class after school while others played sports, but I didn't really fit into that category.

If you start a blog, it gives you something to do besides browse the TV Guide or pick up the video game controller. Not only are you doing something different, but it's super productive. When people ask you what you did last week or over the summer, you can feel good about telling them you started a blog.

5) Be accountable for something

We're going to cover this in detail later, but it's pretty important to regularly post on a blog. The best way to be successful is to keep up with it. That means that you have to be accountable.

When you're young, it can be easy to rely on other people — mom or dad make dinner, they drive you to school, and they pay for most (or all) of your expenses. When you have a blog, it gives you something to be accountable for. It fills your life up with an extra layer of meaning — if you don't check and update your blog, it will fail. It can be nice to finally be in charge of something that's *yours*.

A Blog's Structure

If you're a total newbie, keep reading to understand what exactly makes up a blog. If you're a pro, skip on to the next section.

Every blog consists of the following:

Title: Provides the blog reader with an idea of what the blog is about.

Date: Blogs are displayed in reverse chronological order, so the most recent post is at the top.

Post Title: The title of each blog post.

Blog Text: This is the actual text that each blog post consists of.

About: This is information about the individual or business that actually wrote the blog (sometimes, this contains contact information).

Comments: This is an area for the readers to place comments, responses, opinions, or reactions to a blog post. You don't have to have this on your blog if you don't want it, but that's part of the blog's charm.

Previous Blog Posts: This is the reverse chronological listing of previous blog posts from most recent to oldest.

Archived Posts: Even the best blogs get bulky; it is not uncommon to archive old posts after a preset period of time.

Blogroll: A list of links to other related sites.

Advertising: This is a common sight in the world of blogging. Many advertisements are prominently featured (typically in free blogging applications). In some cases, you can generate revenue through the use of advertising, but often, this is third party advertisements that you allow for use of the free blogging software.

Choosing the Best Blogging Software

In today's day and age, there are three major blogging platforms: WordPress.com, Blogger, and Tumblr. You can go with any of these options and be successful, but for the sake of covering all the bases, let's briefly compare them.

WordPress.com

This blogging platform is free to use unless you want to upgrade to the paid version. If you don't want to throw in any money to start out with, then this is a pretty awesome option. This is the most popular, most widely used program.

Pros: It's free to start and it's really user-friendly. You don't need to be a computer expert to figure this one out. If you're a pro at coding, that's cool, but it's not necessary for this platform. You also have a ton of different layouts to choose from. Some of them cost, but there are a lot of free ones, and they look very professional and sleek.

Cons: You can't really customize a layout unless you want to pay. Once you choose your fav, you're stuck with what you get. Also, you don't technically own your blog, which means WordPress gets to advertise on your behalf. They also have the power to shut down your blog if they want. Which would stink. A lot.

Blogger

This one is also free, and Google owns it, so you get all the Google perks (AdSense and Analytics). This one is also really easy to use, so pretty much anyone can start up a blog.

Pros: It's free, it's easy to use, and you can make easy money through Google AdSense.

Cons: You don't have as many theme options as WordPress. You also don't own your site, so you're pretty dependent on Blogger.

Note: For both WordPress and Blogger, you'll have the fancy ".wordpress.com" and ".blogspot.com" in your URL. That can be a con for some people who don't want that association front and center.

Tumblr

Also free, this site is really good for people who want to be social. It's more of a social media site than it is a blogging site, because the emphasis is on reblogging material.

Pros: You have unlimited storage space, so you don't have to worry about running out of room. There are also a ton of themes to choose from — over 1,000 — so you're bound to find something you love.

Cons: It's pretty tough to make money on Tumblr. It's also pretty hard to import content from other places. You also can't really do longer posts, because this platform is based on posts that are short and sweet.

There are other blogging options, but they aren't as popular as these. The other ones are also not ideal for a young adult to use — some are better for businesses. The other options are: TypePad, Wix, Quora, Squarespace and LinkedIn. There are even more beyond these, but these are some of the ones you might recognize.

Who Blogs?

Obviously, a critical component to the success of any blog is who will participate in the blog. A blog is nothing without participation from subscribers and readers. After all, if a tree falls in the forest and no one is there to hear it fall, does the tree even exist?

Anyone can blog. You can be Perez Hilton or a kindergartener on your mom's iPad — seriously, anyone can do it. Blogging has exploded in popularity and is now considered the communications method of the future.

☞ *Fast Fact:*

Nine-year-old Martha Payne posted what she was given to eat at school one day (a slice of pizza and a single potato croquette). Her dad posted and tweeted about it, and three hours later, her blog had more than 10,000 visitors. Her blog has been viewed nine million times, it landed her a book deal, and it has raised a ton of money for Mary's Meals, a charity (The Telegraph 2013).

Blogging is much more than just a journal — it can actually be a huge marketing tool. Sure, you might not want to start a blog for your business (you can, you overachiever, you), but you can think bigger when it comes to blogging. The Internet holds so much opportunity, and the blogging world really stands at the forefront of that chance.

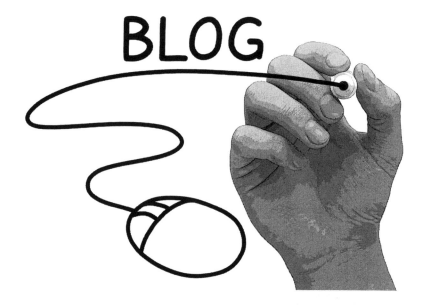

As we embark on our journey toward establishing a blog, keep in mind the primary principal of blogging: Instead of publishing static information, you are participating in an online conversation. You want bloggers to talk to you, which means that you should really be posting content that can be talked about.

Long story short: Who blogs? Anyone and everyone.

Understanding Pingbacks and Trackbacks

If you have no clue what those words mean, don't worry. They aren't confusing — they're a super cool feature of blogging. "Trackbacks and pingbacks" allow readers to link directly to your blog posts and recommend your blog to others.

Trackbacks are simply an announcement method between blogs. It allows a blog reader to send a notice to someone else that the blog might be something they would have an interest in reading. It's just like a YouTube response video if you've ever noticed those.

Here's an example:

> I publish something in my blog about my next book title — the post is called "My Next Book."

>> One of my blog readers, Gary, sees this and decides to leave a comment. In addition to letting other viewers see his comment, he also wants to allow them to comment about "My Next Book" on his blog, too.

>>> Another blog reader, Charlie, posts something on his blog and sends a trackback to my blog.

>>>> I receive the trackback and display it in the form of a comment on my blog, along with the link back to the blog reader's post on his blog.

Still with me?

Anyone who reads blogs can follow the trackback to my blog and vice versa.

Why is this important? This is how blogging is unique from websites and discussion forums. The theory is that blog readers from both blogs can read the blog posts and, ultimately, more people would join in on the whole shebang.

The problem with trackbacks is that they can be spammed or spoofed easily, and there is no real authentication process to make sure that a trackback is valid. This is where pingbacks come in.

Pingbacks are sent automatically when you link to someone's site or when they link to yours. If your blog post has a link to the blog that you're hoping to connect with when you post, then you don't need to send a trackback to alert them.

Here's an example:

> I publish something in my blog about my next book title —
> the post is called "My Next Book."

>> One of my blog readers, Gary, sees this and decides to
>> leave a comment. In addition to letting other viewers see
>> his comment, he also wants to allow them to comment
>> about "My Next Book" on his blog, too.

>>> The blog reader, Charlie, posts something on his blog
>>> and links back to my blog.

>>>> Charlie's blogging software automatically sends a
>>>> notification to me, telling me that my blog has been
>>>> linked to. My blog software automatically includes
>>>> this information about the link in my blog.

Confused? It can be hard to tell the difference between the two, because they both accomplish the same thing. Here are the differences:

- They use different technologies to communicate.

- Pingbacks are automated, while trackbacks are manual.

- Trackbacks send the comments; pingbacks do not. Trackbacks typically send only part of your comments to intrigue the reader into following the actual links to read the entire blog or blog entries.

- Pingbacks appear as links only. Trackbacks appear as links with some content/comments.

- Trackbacks can be faked, spoofed, and spammed. Pingbacks are not easily faked.

- Trackbacks provide the reader with a preview of the content on the blog, whereas pingbacks do not.

Overall, trackbacks and pingbacks are another way to get people to look at your blog — the more, the merrier.

Okay, so you're well versed in what a blog is, who does it, and how the basic functions of trackbacking and pingbacking work. Let's move on to your mom's favorite chapter — blogging etiquette. But, first! Let's hear from an expert.

FROM THE EXPERTS:
MERYL K. EVAN

"Blog" today is the "email" of 10 years ago: More people know about blogs, but don't necessarily use it or plan to in the future.

Here are the five tips to building a better blog — you might think some of these are "duh" or "common sense ideas," but after surfing hundreds and maybe even thousands of blogs, these mistakes appeared again and again. We should be making other mistakes with our blogs — new mistakes — not these five.

1. Small Banner

If you can't see the content without scrolling, then your banner (also referred to as a header) is too big. This valuable screen estate is known as the active window or "above the fold." Your site only has a few seconds to prove itself and hiding the goods below the fold lowers your chances of getting someone to stick around.

While scrolling up and down is rarely a big deal, a reader might not want to bother scrolling when casually browsing blogs or websites. Why take the chance? As I surfed from blog to blog, I wanted a snapshot of the page as soon as I arrived. I'm busy. I've got sites to go to and sites to see: I'm not going to make an effort to crawl around for content. Banners are meaningless when they take up too much screen estate.

2. Short Articles

Some blogs consistently have content with over 800 words. Shoot for around 500 words or fewer. Save the longer stuff for newsletters, magazines, and other appropriate outlets. Also, use bold face type and bolded headers in the longer articles to help readers with scanning.

While the occasional long entry is okay, doing it on a regular basis doesn't impress. Instead, it drags. Readers want to read the heart of the content and get out. They don't want to spend time on a blog entry when there are thousands of blogs out there. Multiply thousands of blogs with hundreds of entries and you've got a winning recipe for information overload.

When you do post a longer than normal entry, consider posting an excerpt of the entry on the home page rather than the whole entry. If a reader wants to read more, then she can click for the rest of the article. If not, the next entry is further up the screen trying to entice the reader to stick around just a little longer.

3. Readable

Obvious? Not according to the hundreds of blogs I've visited. While bright colors may be cool to tweens and teens, they ain't cool for serious blogs. Not only are colors a problem, but so is font size. How many times have you heard someone complain, "The font is too big?" If I have to squint, then I'm not visiting again. We can use our browser's options to change the font size, but it won't work for all sites. Giving font size control to readers lets them figure out what works best for them. You may have selected a reasonable font size, but browsers, Macs versus PCs, and monitor resolution settings can shrink it. Text Sizing shows how text looks in different browsers and different PCs.

While browsers like Firefox (which I use as my primary browser) can change text on websites with fonts that can't be changed, not everyone uses Firefox nor do they know how to change the text size using their browser's options.

Also, use italics sparingly. Many people have trouble reading words in italics. If you often quote resources and they're more than a paragraph long, it might be better to use quotation marks, indentation, or both.

Italics slow down reading, give us headaches, and create a difficult reading experience as we squint, dragging our cursor over the content in attempt to see it better when it's selected (or copy it into a word processor).

Speaking of difficult to read, a terrible trend has come to light that doesn't show signs of slowing down. I'm guilty of this with Bionic Ear because I was too lazy to change the template: Gray text on white. Gray has become the new black, and stylish it's not! Stop it! Don't make me start a "GRAY Group: Gray reads awful, y'all!" Dorky, I know, but change the font to "#000000" or "black," and you won't ever hear me speak of GRAY Group again.

4. Frequent

When a blog isn't regularly updated, why should people come back to it, bookmark it, or save the feed? They don't.

After all, there are many more blogs out there where the bloggers make the time to update at least two or three times a week. While a CEO of a big company might be an exception from frequent posting, it doesn't apply to most of us.

5. Silent

Arriving on a blog and getting greeted with music can freak out the reader especially if he doesn't share the blogger's taste in music. In most cases, there is no way to turn off the music from within the site. Even if you have audio entries or podcasts, I've yet to see a blog where an audio entry started without my help.

Think about your least favorite type of music. What would you do if you heard it when you arrived on a blog?

Even though I don't have perfect hearing, unexpected music in a blog has sent me jumping out of my Aeron chair (it really works for me) a few times and not for good reason.

In addition, many surfers are in an office or other public setting as well. Not all of them have headphones plugged into the PC and get embarrassed when music starts blasting out of the blue especially if they're on a conference call or are checking a personal blog during work time (not that any of us do that!).

Meryl K. Evans, Content Maven behind meryl.net, has written and edited for AbsoluteWrite, ECT News Network, The Dallas Morning News, Digital Web, Lockergnome, MarketingProfs, PC Today, O'Reilly, Pearson, Sams, Wiley, and WROX. She has written copy for businesses as well as Fib-or-Not? and Meet, Mix, and Mingle games. She is Editor-in-Chief of

Shavlik's The Remediator Security Digest, a popular newsletter on computer security with over 100,000 subscribers.

She's also the editor of Professional Service Journal, an email newsletter for business-to-business service providers, Intel Solution Services' Connected Digest, and TailoredMail's Focus eJournal. Meryl's the author of Brilliant Outlook Pocketbooks. Meryl is an educator with New York University's online graduate program.

She has worked for two Fortune 500 telecom companies, the U.S. federal government in Washington, D.C. and IT consulting. A native Texan, she lives a heartbeat north of Dallas in Plano, Texas with her husband and three kiddos.

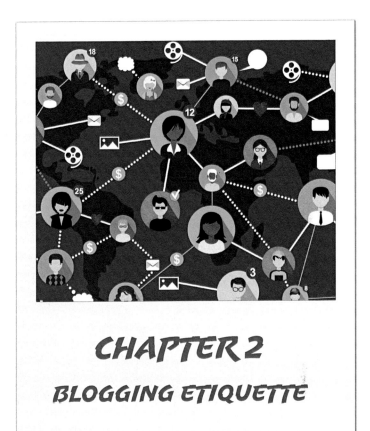

CHAPTER 2
BLOGGING ETIQUETTE

The blogosphere has developed informal rules and behavior protocols to follow. This is very similar to what many refer to as "man code." While it might seem silly to cover blogging etiquette (you can really do whatever you want), it may be worthwhile to take a look through this chapter. A fact of life for serious bloggers is that, if you don't play by the rules, your blog will lose readers.

In no particular order, here are our best pieces of blogging etiquette advice.

The Golden Rule

The golden rule with blogs, especially corporate or organizational blogs, is to **stay on topic**. This can feel constraining, but people gravitate toward blogs that emit a singular purpose. For example, if you want fashion advice, you'll be sure to check out Hello Fashion, Atlantic Pacific, or Style Me Gracie. If one of these blogs randomly posted about cars or sports, you'd probably be confused, right?

So, if you decide to skip the rest of this chapter (don't!), just remember that choosing a main topic is the most important part of your blog's success.

☞ _Fast Fact:_

There's a blog called "Lonely Cheetos."
You can browse through an extensive photo collection of Cheetos that fell on the ground.
You can also send in your pictures:
http://lonelycheetos.tumblr.com.

Don't Be a Simpleton

Okay, so we really just like the word simpleton. But, in all seriousness, your blog is public. It's out there for anyone to read. Although you may only be targeting a specific audience, everyone can read it and post comments. Your blog represents you — make sure you're being appropriate and are sending the message you want to.

It's Not About You

A blog isn't really for you — it's for your readers. So, write for the reader. You need to be captivating, interesting, and, most of all, relevant to something they are interested in or care about. If you don't carefully consider what your readers want and need, no one will read your blog. And if no one hears the tree fall…

Prepare for the Best

Expect positive comments on your blog. When you get them, take the time to thank the individual.

Prepare for the Worst

Expect spam comments. Expect negative, argumentative, and insulting comments. Many bloggers are jerks (for lack of a better word — maybe simpleton is better?). They thrive on spreading the gospel of hate, stupidity, and ignorance. You can edit these comments out, but that's really time consuming.

Kill the jerks with kindness, stay relevant, stick to your ground rules, and push your main message. You won't make everyone happy all the time, so don't even try. For the ones that go totally psycho, ban them.

Create a Routine

Update your blog on a regular basis. If you update daily, you should stick to that routine. If you can't commit to that, do it weekly. Your readers will expect updates on a periodic basis. If you tell them your blog will be updated daily, but it never is, they will quickly lose interest.

Many famous and successful bloggers announce their routine, whatever it may be, and they stick to it. For example, beauty blogger Tati (2.3 million subscribers) uploads a new video on YouTube every weekday around 9 a.m. Other bloggers don't have that kind of time — beauty blogger NikkiTutorials (5.8 million subscribers) uploads a new video every Wednesday and Sunday at 4 p.m.

In other words, how consistent you are matters more than how often you're actually posting.

☞ *Fast Fact:*

"Blogs that post daily get 5x more traffic compared to those that don't" (Jatain 2015).

Don't be a Plagiarizer

When reproducing an article or something someone else has written, get permission.

If you are including information from another blog or are discussing topics that are referenced on another blog you will be discussing, ensure that you put a link to the original source.

You should not steal website content and post it in your blog (unless you have permission to do so). You should not take images from a website and embed them in your blog. It is acceptable, however, to link to an image on another site or blog.

Don't Exploit your Friends

Always respect the privacy of your friends. Don't start making posts about your friend's eating habits or how your sister never cleans the toilet (especially if they don't know about it). There is nothing wrong with public opinion, praise, and recognition of others. That's actually pretty awesome. But don't go posting your ex-girlfriend's phone number on your blog telling people to prank call her. That's not cool.

Connect with Other Blogs

Add blogs you read regularly to your blogroll. A blogroll is a blogger's list of his favorite blogs. Add the ones that matter to you most. It's nice to have blogs link to you, and it's nice to know who it is. Again, this is open for debate, but stick to adding your favorites and the most popular, and you won't go wrong.

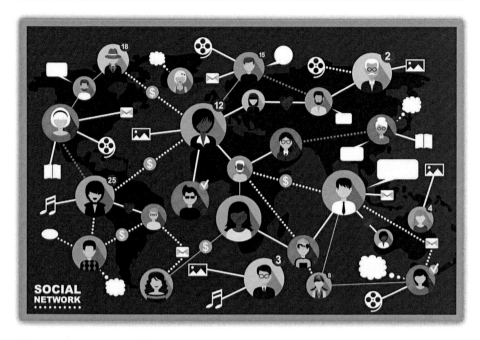

Put on Your Grammar Cap

You should correct typos and errors in your blogs. This doesn't mean editing comments you don't really like or don't agree with. This is strictly to correct grammatical or typographical errors.

> ☞ *Fast Fact:*
>
> Coke makes four times fewer writing mistakes than Pepsi in its posts on LinkedIn (Conner 2013).

What Would Grandma Say?

Do not write anything you do not want anyone else to know about. If you write it, it may come back to haunt you later. Don't write anything you wouldn't want your grandmother to see. You know exactly what we mean.

Again, there are no hard and fast rules.

Go with the rule of respect and common sense, and you can't go wrong.

FROM THE EXPERTS: JUSTIN PREMICK

Education Marketing Manager,
AWeber Communications —
www.aweber.com

1. Do Unto Others...

This is probably the first and most important rule in blogging just as much as anywhere else.

Part of why you start a blog is to humanize your organization, and when you do that, you (as the voice of that organization) implicitly agree to abide by the same social rules and conventions that you would as an individual.

Break those rules, and you'll pay the consequences — plenty of your readers have their own blogs, and should you treat them discourteously, the rest of the Internet will know all about it.

2. Don't Hide

This goes hand-in-hand with #1. If someone writes something bad about you, in a comment on your blog or on his or her own blog, don't avoid the conversation. Engage them in conversation and find out what's behind the disagreement. After all, you got into blogging to communicate, right?

If you do choose to moderate your comments (and we do here at AWeber), don't censor! If someone says something about you or your organization that you don't like, keeping it from showing up in a comment on your own blog just means it's going to appear on their blog, in detail.

That said, if someone's being abusive, there are times when it serves both of you better to talk in person, either via email or phone, prior to approving or removing such a comment. The right to free speech does not guarantee the right to an audience, and if someone is intentionally trying to trash you, you're under no obligation to allow that to happen on your blog.

3. Stand For Something

Not everyone's going to agree with you or like you. If they do, they're probably bored with you.

Don't try to be everything to everyone. Know who you are, express your viewpoints, and be prepared to stand by them. If you change a stance, do it because you believe it's the right move, not because someone pressured you into it. Again, blogging imitates life here.

Being provocative is not a bad thing, especially if you're provoking a discussion among your readers. They won't all agree, but some of them will, and they'll all respect you for your frankness.

4. Publish or Perish

You don't necessarily have to say, "we're going to blog every Monday, Wednesday, and Friday" — but you DO need to put out content consistently. Otherwise, people will lose interest and find other places to interact. Remember, your blog is a community shared by you and your readers. Neglect that community, and it will fall apart.

Located in Newtown, PA, AWeber Communications develops and manages online opt-in email newsletters, follow-up automation, and email deliverability services for small business customers around the world. Customers access our website 24/7 to manage and send their newsletters to recipients who have specifically opted in on their website to receive that information.

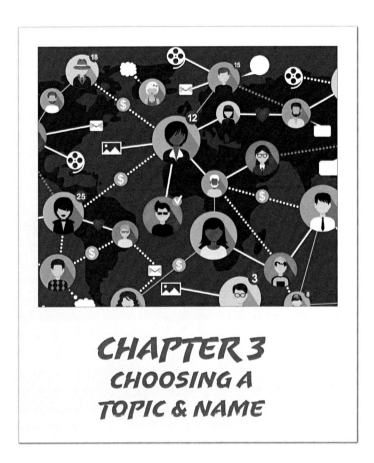

CHAPTER 3
CHOOSING A
TOPIC & NAME

There is an art to blogging and an art to blogging effectively. Finding your niche can be pretty difficult—there's so many different subjects to choose from. This chapter will help you discover where your passions are and how to turn those passions into an eye-catching name that takes over the internet. OK, maybe not a name that takes over the internet, but at least a name that has a nice ring to it. Read on to find your niche.

What Should I Blog About?

A good blog entertains, enlightens, captures interest, fascinates, sparks debate, and inspires conversation. A blog needs to be unique, invigorating, and useful.

Since there are millions of blogs out there, you need to be unique. Why is someone going to look at your food blog when there's another, more popular blogger talking about the same things?

It can be difficult to find your place in the blogging world, but to get started, let's get your creative juices flowing with 50 ideas. If one of these topics seems like something you're interested in, start thinking about how you can add something unique to the subject area.

1. Self improvement
2. Health/fitness
3. Travel
4. Animals
5. Personal development
6. Communication skills
7. Self-defense
8. Recipes
9. Technology
10. Bullying
11. Tutorials
12. DIY projects
13. Relationship advice
14. Friend advice
15. Career/jobs
16. Finance
17. Ghost-hunting
18. Video games
19. Gardening
20. Social media
21. Photography
22. Blog & website tips
23. Confidence & self-esteem
24. Self-employment
25. How to write well
26. Interior design
27. Life skills for high school/college students
28. Sports
29. Public speaking
30. Meditation
31. Family
32. Musical instruments
33. Music in general
34. Movie reviews
35. Book reviews
36. Music reviews
37. Simple living
38. History
39. Politics
40. Celebrities
41. Tourism
42. Shopping
43. Fashion
44. Beauty
45. Makeup
46. Product reviews
47. Parodies
48. Jokes
49. Interviews
50. News

☞ *Fast Fact:*

The three most popular blogs of all time are Huffington Post (news), TMZ (celebrities), and Business Insider (business).

The list doesn't end here — what are you good at? What interests you? When you get home from school, what's the first thing you get excited about? That might be your perfect starting point.

What's in a Name?

If you haven't chosen your topic yet, that's all right. If you have, you might be ready to start thinking about creating a title for your blog. Titles attract attention. Make them capture the essence of your blog. If you fail to capture attention with your blog title, readers won't flock to you.

Keep in mind that good titles drive your overall readership. Most people scan Web pages and only stop when something catches their attention. If your title doesn't do that, you will lose potential followers.

Step 1: Do some comps

If you've ever heard of the term "comps," it has probably been related to real estate. Realtors generally take a look at houses similar to yours, and then they tell you how much yours is worth based on those comparables.

Well, you want to do the same thing when you're choosing a name for your blog. I'm going to use our blog as an example because it really fits this piece of advice well.

Topic: We want to create a blog for teens and young adults that are interested in nonfiction books — we want to create a place where they can interact with us and start discussions.

What we're starting with: The name of our publishing company is Atlantic Publishing Group, Inc. That's all we really have to work with at this point.

What everyone else in our niche is doing: Well, we did a Facebook search for the three biggest publishing companies in the world — Penguin Random House, Simon & Schuster, and HarperCollins. Here's what their young adult Facebook pages are called:

- Penguin Teen
- SimonTEEN
- HarperTeen

Our name became clear just from looking at the comps.

Final name: AtlanticTeen.

You won't always have this kind of crazy-good luck, but it can be important to see what else is out there for other reasons, too. You don't want to start up a blog called LifeHacks just to find out that one of the most popular blogs in the world is called LifeHacker.

You also want to see what kinds of things they're talking about. You don't want to double them — try to find your niche. You can use their posts as inspiration for your own, but if you post the same things, no one will find your blog necessary.

Step 2: Make a list of keywords

If you aren't fortunate enough to have a company name to start out with, you're starting from absolute scratch. In this scenario, it's really helpful to sit down and make a list of words associated with your topic. For example, if your topic is music, you might write words like these: rhythm, beats, melody, tune, acoustic, soul, fusion, refrain, song, lyric, chime, descant, resonance, musicality, and so on.

If you can't think of anything and you're staring at a blank piece of paper, hop on to **www.thesaurus.com** and start looking for synonyms. Even the most creative of people get stuck.

Once you have your list made up, scan through it and look for words that appeal to you. Maybe it's the way the word looks on the page, the way it sounds, or the connotations it has — try to think of how you could use that word in a title.

Step 3: Make a list of possible names

So many lists, we know, but once you start brainstorming actual names, write every single one of them down. Try to crank out at least 15 names. It doesn't matter how stupid you think they sound — you might find that mixing and matching a few of the names brings you to the winner.

When you have a huge list, whittle them down by crossing out the ones you know you don't love. When you can come down to a select few, run them by friends and family. They might notice something that you don't —a strange affiliation with a word, a double meaning you didn't notice, or even the fact that it sounds funny when you say it out loud.

Once you have everyone's input, you should have a winner on your hands! Do a quick Web search to make sure it doesn't already exist. You wouldn't want to double someone else, especially if the name is trademarked or copyrighted.

Top 5 Strangest Blogs

1. Breaded Cats
   (**www.breadedcats.com**)

2. Hungover Owls
   (**http://hungoverowls.tumblr.com**)

3. Accidental Chinese Hipsters
   (**http://accidentalchinesehipsters.tumblr.com**)

4. Men Taking Up Too Much Space on the Train
   (**http://mentakingup2muchspaceonthetrain. tumblr.com**)

5. Kim Jong-Il Looking at Things
   (**http://kimjongillookingatthings.tumblr.com**)

FROM THE EXPERTS:
EMILY ROBBINS

Find her at:
www.emilyrobbins.com/how-to-blog.

So, you want to start a new blog. Maybe you don't have much experience with blogging, so you don't think it's that big of a deal which platform you choose or whether you have your own domain name. Well, think again.

Don't fall victim to the disaster that I landed myself in, where I started casually blogging and ended up regularly blogging and hating the platform I was using but can't easily switch because I stupidly put my blog on a subdomain of TypePad (**http://blogging.typepad.com**).

Now I'm at TypePad's mercy. They own my behind because they own my address — even though I'm paying $150+ a year for their service. The same could happen to you whether it's a subdomain on **typepad. com**, **blogspot.com**, or **wordpress.com**.

By not having your own domain name, if you ever decide to move to another blogging platform you run the risk of losing all (or a lot) of your traffic, your search engine rankings, all of your hard earned incoming links, etc. because you cannot take your URL with you.

How are you going to redirect your traffic to your new blog when you have NO ability to, say, set up a 301 Permanent Redirect? Which, for those who are wondering, would both:

- Automatically redirect human visitors to your new blog site
- Tell the search engines that your blog has permanently moved and gives it the new location

Domain names are cheap — about $9 a year for a single one, as low as $6.75 a year if you own more than 50. There is NO excuse to not have your own domain name for your blog. You will regret it at some point down the road if you don't start out with your own domain name.

GoDaddy.com is the site that I use to register my domain names, although there are numerous other options, such as $5.99 domain names at 1&1, and, if you only need a single domain name, the cheapest option is domain names from Yahoo! for only $2.99.

The irony here is that I actually own a lot of domain names and I genuinely can't fathom why I didn't just use a domain of my own when I started my blog.

Just to clarify, my point is that you need to own your own domain name so the URL for your blog points to a domain you own and control. It's okay to use a subdomain off a domain that you own, but not one that belongs to someone else, such as that of a hosted service like **typepad.com**.

And it's okay to use a hosted solution — just make sure you pick one (like typepad.com or blogger.com) that allows you to use your own domain name (and always reference your blog's URL with your own domain) so that if you ever decide you want to go elsewhere, at least you'll be able to take your traffic with you. And it's also a good idea to check to see if whatever blogging platform you start with has the ability to export your posts (and comments/trackbacks) for easiest porting of your site to another platform.

*Emily Robbins created her blog **(www.emilyrobbins.com/how-to-blog)** as she journaled her quest to teach herself how to blog. It has evolved into a blogging how-to guide, with tips and tricks for both new and experienced bloggers. The site includes reviews and comparisons of various blogging platforms, a comprehensive list of over 615 WordPress themes to customize the look and feel of your blog, tutorials for solving specific problems, and much more.*

CHAPTER 4
DESIGN

Design Basics

On one level, blog design is an art form. It's the presentation of a concept or idea through the use of HTML coding, just as a painting is the presentation of an idea using paint. Here are some things to think about when it comes to designing your blog.

Organization

Your readers should never be overwhelmed by the amount of content you have on your homepage. If there's too much information, you'll end up driving people away.

One of the ways you may be able to keep your readers on your blog for the maximum amount of time is by finding some way to establish interactive activities on the site, whether that involves taking part in quizzes and survey polls or posting opinions on message boards. Also think about whether your readers will need to download anything like videos or audio files — that's a really great way to get people to interact with your blog.

Give them what they want

It's important in your design process to have a fairly clear idea of what people want. Since most users have a pretty clear idea of what they expect when they go to a blog, it pays to look closely at what other popular blogs are doing.

For the layout and multimedia content of the blog you design, think about the best way to organize the information you need and the best way to meet the expectations of your visitors. Most sites have a unique homepage layout and two or three secondary page designs.

Uniformity is important as an aesthetic element, too; people don't want to be overwhelmed by too many different page layouts — come up with a fun yet simple homepage, and have one single page design for your blog posts.

Select the best elements — the top three or four page layouts, the best three or four colors, a single font style — and stick with them, applying a single resolution to all the pages.

What do people see?

Just as there are some blogs with too much, there are other blogs that are full of "under construction" pages and black holes. A messy, incomplete page will also steer the average blogger to a better place. For example, if you're using WordPress.com, make sure you fill in all the required information or you'll have a text box at the bottom of your blog that says "Insert Footer 1 Here." Not cute.

So many blogs have amazing content, but they rarely get seen, because they aren't appealing to a user at first glance. Take some time and plot out what you want to do on paper. List all of the links you want to have on your homepage. Color is crucial and should be given plenty of thought. A dark or heavily patterned background with a light text is hard to read and can divert people's attention from your products.

It's worth your time to browse the Web for the most popular companies you can think of. For example, when you look at Apple's homepage, what do you see?

- A clean, white background
- Black text
- The header is above the fold and is very simplistic
- One font is used

You'll notice that less is more — the products are showcased brilliantly because they stand out from the white background.

Top 3 Worst Website Designs (according to Web Pages That Suck)

1. **Riverside Art Center (www.riversideartcenter.org):**
   "As soon as my eyes quit bleeding, I think I shall simply drink heavily. There is no sense in trying to figure out the 'why' of this site. It has all the charm of a junkyard located on top of an old landfill, and right next to a sewage treatment plant."

2. **Preterist Archive (www.preteristarchive.com):**
   "Ah, yes. I have been waiting for another of this genre to show up. For the umpteenth time, I am delighted that this site is so bad, or else someone might take it seriously."

3. **MSY (www.msy.com.au/home.php):**
   "MSY would have made the regular Worst of 2009 list except they changed it enough by the end of the year so I thought the new version didn't qualify so I put it on the Honorary list."

The layout

The layout of your blog can make you or break you. You have limitless options in the layout of your website (well, depending on what platform you use), but there are some general rules to follow that will make your page standard enough for even the extreme novice to use and understand easily.

Avoid making things so busy that no one can focus on a single piece of your blog. Including plenty of space where there is no graphics, text, or links is key to making a website clear and easy to maneuver. If you make it easy for your visitors to completely explore your page without any problems, they will come back for more.

The top of a page should be reserved as a marker for the name of your blog. Think of it as a small billboard or a calling card. You can include a logo (make a logo for yourself with **www.canva. com**). Keep it simple and concise. The best positioning is in the middle third of a page. It will be front and center and impossible not to notice when your homepage loads. Make sure this area is neat, but still has personality and flair to give your blog an identity. Make sure it's not a template or plain text that is boring and seen all around the Web.

Links to other pages on a website, called navigation buttons, are typically positioned in one of three ways. You can place them across the top, down the left side, or down the right side of each page. If you choose, you can place two sets of links at the top and bottom, allowing the visitor to click on links whether they have scrolled all the way down or all the way up the page.

Give your visitors options to increase the likelihood that they will move on to other pages on your site. If you have many different links on your homepage, you may choose to place them vertically on the left or right side just because of how many there are.

A list down either side of the page is much neater than having several that stretch across the screen and out of the main view. If you can limit yourself to one or two lines at the top without having this problem, that is all right. If you have several links, and the top of the page looks like a large block of links clustered together, go with a listing on the side.

Wording

Labels for links should also be short. They should convey the message of what it connects them to without being too wordy. For instance, instead of "All about me and my blogging startup" go with "My Story" or "About Me." Whenever you add a link that is extremely long, the entire page is skewed off of its streamlined look. Keep it short and sweet.

People constantly play a game of "word association," especially when scanning through a site. If they are looking for something in particular, there may be a few words in their head that they are searching for. If someone is looking for information about you as a blogger, they will probably be scanning the page for "Bio," "About Me," or "History." Look at other websites and see what phrases pop up.

It's a good idea to go with the grain. If you want to be unique, you can come up with your own words, but make sure that people can make the connection you intend.

Choosing your fonts

There are many free fonts available online. Choosing the right fonts and using them in the right places can really add to the style of a page. Be creative with titles, but be sure to choose a simple and easily readable font for the main text of the page.

The choice of font size is another important aspect of design. Size 24 is commonly accepted as a good size for headlines, and size 12 is common for regular text. Keep your audience in mind when choosing the font size. Font sizes should be relative. If your main text is going to be in a bigger text, then the headline must be much larger. The standard ratio between the body text and the title text is two to three times larger. Titles that are too large will attract attention, but it will seem unprofessional in nature. This is similar to the difference between tabloid headlines and newspaper headlines.

5 Most Used Fonts of 2015 (Typewolf.com)

1. **Futura**

2. **Aperçu**

3. **Proxima Nova**

4. **Gotham**

5. **Brown**

Design Mistakes

Avoid these common design mistakes!

A lackluster home page

You should be able to visit the home page of any website and figure out what the site is about, what type of products it sells, or what it is advertising within about five seconds. The same goes for your blog — when you visit it, you should immediately have a clear idea of what your topic is.

If your name doesn't indicate it, make sure you have some kind of subtitle or tagline that explains it. For example, our blog, AtlanticTeen, has a headline that says, "Tuning you in to the young adult nonfiction book world."

Popup windows

The poor use of popup windows, splashy advertising, splash pages (pages with neat animations and sound but which you have to watch for five to ten seconds before you are taken to the real website), and other design features that draw interest away from your blog should be avoided altogether.

Bad direction

Nothing is worse than going to a website and having no clue where to go — this includes broken hyperlinks, hidden navigation, poor wording of navigational links, links which take you to pages with no links, and links from a page to the same Web page and no links back to the home page (whew!). Always include a link back to the home page so that regardless of where a site visitor goes, they can find their way back home.

Outdated content

There is nothing more dissatisfying to a reader than visiting a blog that is completely out-of-date.

Make sure you're constantly updating posts as well as your contact information. If you get a new email address, make sure you update it on your blog. If you aren't doing that giveaway every month anymore, update your schedule of events. It doesn't take a reader long to realize that your blog hasn't been updated since before the last presidential election, and typically, interest fades fast.

Misusing text

Forget flashing text, reversing text, gymnastics text, or other eye-popping and dizzying effects, which do nothing more than annoy your visitors. Don't create a "loud" website that contains so many blinking, flashing, twirling, and spinning icons, text, or graphics — visitors will be overwhelmed by the effects and underwhelmed by the site content. Here is a great example of a website that is out of control: **http://arngren.net**.

Overusing capitalization

Most people today know and understand basic Web communication, which means that if you choose to use capitalized words in your emails and chats, your readers might feel as if you are yelling at them.

On the Web, you can easily offend people by using capital letters to make a point. SO UNLESS THIS IS YOUR INTENT, USE CAPITALIZATION CAREFULLY AND SPARINGLY IN ALL COMMUNICATIONS WITH YOUR VISITORS. There are tons of ways to draw visitors to specific areas of your blog without resorting to capitalization.

Blog Content

Content drives search engine visibility and is vitally important to achieving success on the Web. Content is critical not only in drawing visitors to your site, but also in getting them to return time and time again. Writing solid, comprehensible content means two things: You have to know your topic, and you have to have a good grasp of how to build your content into something of value.

Search engines look for well-written, interesting, and unique content that is updated and relevant.

Writing the content

Content should be written so that it can be easily scanned, because site visitors may not have time to read super thick paragraphs. Include bold-faced headlines with text to make it easier for visitors to find what they're looking for without having to read everything.

The lede

The first sentence and paragraph of your posts will determine whether your visitors will read the entire blog post. One of the first things you learn in journalism is how to write a lede, which is that first sentence you see in most newspaper stories. It must be something that grabs the reader's attention and is best served with a solid verb to describe what the article is about.

Here are a few examples of good ledes from **Poynter.org**:

- "The babies showed up on Craigslist at 1:26 p.m., May 6."

- "The downfall of a cocaine kingpin and one-time enforcer for a violent Mexican drug cartel began at the bottom of a Pike Creek trash can."

- "In a flash of fire, it became less a matter of space than of heaven."

- "It's all around you, all the time. Tidily rolled up next to the toilet when you wake up in the morning, handed to you at the corner cafe with your morning coffee, all over your desk at work, and surrounding much of the food you buy at the grocery store before heading home."

Relevance and spell-checking

Make sure your content is not only timely but also relevant to your readers. Remember to spell-check everything. Do it as you write and again when you are finished. Also make sure to check your grammar closely.

The flow

Another factor to remember is to leave enough space between your content and graphics or images. Don't let your content flow under or over these items. If you have content that is buried or unreadable, you'll annoy your readers, and you may lose current and future subscribers, because the site looks unprofessional.

How users read the content

People rarely read anything word for word; instead, they sweep the page, selecting various words and sentences. In researching on the way in which people read websites, it was discovered that only 16 percent read word-for-word. Consequently, Web pages must use analyzable text and employ accentuated key words. Web pages also must contain significant sub-headings, bulleted lists, and ideas organized by paragraph.

Using Images

The use of images and visual impact is necessary in order to seize the attention of site visitors. You must gain their attention immediately, and the creative use of images is one of the best ways to do that.

Keep in mind that the content is what is most important. Unlike window shopping, visual appeal of a blog will not get attention; someone must be searching on keywords to find your page. But the images you use will complement your content and provide a balanced presentation of your blog. Images should be used strictly to enhance your content.

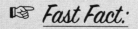

☞ Fast Fact:

Blog posts with images get 94% more views compared to those without them (Jatain 2015).

Excessive use of images characterizes a page as a hobbyist or entertainment page, while reserved use of images is usually correlated with information and news-related sites. They can be used to set the tone of an article through pictures and photographs. They can also be used to enhance the style of a website through advanced graphics techniques to mimic a three-dimensional look or to create effects of reflection.

General advice

Using images on your blog can be tricky — here are a few, general pieces of advice to make sure your images are successful.

Use three graphics per page

Most Web masters believe the rule of thumb is to use no more than three pictures or graphics on any given page, and resize them to no more than 72 DPI, or dots per inch, to ensure they load quickly. Space out images so that the written content is clearly visible on the page, which allows your visitors the opportunity to begin reading your content as the pictures load. Be cautious with the sizing of your fonts — too large a font is not professional and is distracting; too small, and it cannot be easily read.

Ditch clipart — opt for royalty-free stock photos

Clipart should be used with extreme caution because it tends to make your site look amateurish in nature. Most of the clipart and graphics available for free download are low quality. One of the best blog investments you can make is to sign up for royalty-free stock photos. These can add a touch of class and provide a visual center of interest on an otherwise plain Web page.

Placement

The eyes of visitors often tend to travel to four critical points that are all one third of the way from the edges of the page. Place advertisements or other important content in these regions to gain maximum visibility. This rule also applies to the composition of an image. Place the important subjects of the image at these points to make them more noticeable at first glance.

Simplicity

Simple and usable is always better than stylish and complex when it comes to websites. Take a look at the Google homepage. The clean user interface allows first-time users to navigate the site and access its features without any trouble. Simplicity also helps with loading time and bandwidth, since there is less data to be sent and received. It reduces the strain on the user as well as the Web developer or Web host. Users will always prefer sites that are easy to use over the more complex alternatives. Simplicity sells.

Think from the perspective of the website user. What would they want from your site? What information are they looking for? All of the images, graphics, and design elements of the site should be focused around the content.

You also need to be aware that most users are looking at your blog from their phone — whatever blogging platform you decide to use will let you do a "mobile preview." Make sure that everything is clear and well organized. If it isn't — get to work!

> ☞ *Fast Fact:*
>
> Smartphones and tablets now account for 60% of total time spent online (Jatain 2015). 78 percent of the users looking at our Facebook page (**www.facebook.com/AtlanticTeen**) are looking from their phones.

Color Schemes

When choosing a color scheme, keep the feeling you want to create for the website in mind. The choice of colors is usually a personal one, as everyone has his or her own individual preferences regarding color. However, different colors have different connotations; let's take a look at the meaning behind different color schemes.

Warm colors

Warm colors such as red, orange, and yellow can represent passion, energy, excitement, and happiness. Red backgrounds are used to emphasize white text on a page, and red is favored for advertisements and drawing attention to a particular section of a website.

> ☞ *Fast Fact:*
>
> Pink suppresses anger and anxiety. That's why you see some prisons painting their cells and walls pink.

Orange is a great color to use as it is warm, yet it draws the eye's attention to it and offers a bold contrast to other colors. Yellows are warm, cheerful, and soft and offer softer tones to other bolder colors; it's great for contrast.

Cool colors

Cool colors like blue, green, purple, and violet are used to create a sense of peace and serenity. They represent water, nature, and night and offer soothing and relaxing properties. These are ideal colors to give balance and stability to a blog's overall appearance.

Neutral colors

Softer, neutral colors are created when the colors are closer together (Ex: 255, 200, 150). These should be used mainly for backgrounds and other large, solid-colored spaces. Shades of gray are created when the red, green, and blue values are all the same (Ex: 127, 127, 127). Neutral colors are pleasing to the eye and give a natural, balanced appearance. Other colors such as brights and neons tend to cause eye fatigue and drive customers away due to sensory overload.

Neon

Bright neon colors are created when one value is a lot higher than the two others (Ex: Neon Green: 0, 255, 0). Excessive use of neon colors is often considered an eye sore. I do not recommend using excessively bright or neon colors, nor do I recommend animation on Web pages, as it causes fatigue and confusion and will drive readers away.

Integrating color

Use colors that are adjacent to each other to create a sense of consistency to your blog. Use colors that are opposite of each other in the color wheel to highlight content by making it stand out. Over-contrasting everything could become an eye sore, so be picky in choosing what to emphasize.

The colors on the foreground of the page should be at the opposite end of the color wheel so they are easily visible against the background. Red text on a red colored background is unreadable, while green or blue text can be easily read on the same page. Look around at other websites to find complimentary images and colors. Keep in mind that you can't go wrong with black and white.

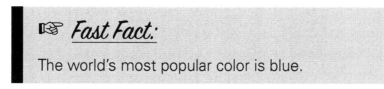

☞ *Fast Fact:*

The world's most popular color is blue.

Accessibility for vision-impaired users is another factor to consider when choosing a color scheme. While red text on a green background (or vice versa) stands out easily, it can sometimes be hard to read due to excessive contrast. To fix this problem, simply adjust the lightness of the colors so that the foreground is darker and the background is lighter. Easy readability is especially a concern if your website is for an elderly audience.

There are lots of resources available to help you with color palettes and Web design including **www.color-wheel-pro. com/color-meaning.html** and **vanseodesign.com/web-design/ color-meaning**.

Navigation

The most common navigation "styles" are explained below with image examples.

HTML links: Simple, efficient and great for search engines. Not as appealing as fancy buttons or other methods.

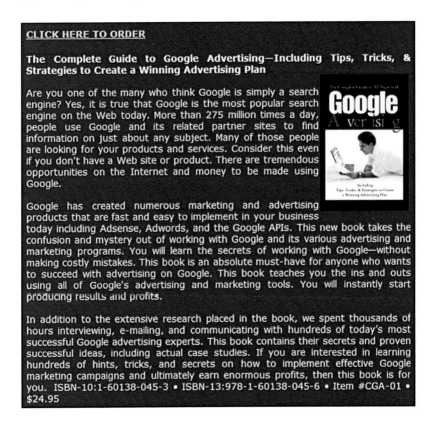

Breadcrumb trail: This system uses a single line of text to show a page's location in the site hierarchy. This should only be used as a secondary navigation system, however it is very useful to the site visitor to show where they are in a website's hierarchy.

Back to: Technology / Calculators & Office Machines

Navigation bars/buttons: By far the most common type of navigation. Typically found on the left hand side of a Web page or across the top of a Web page.

Tab navigation: First made popular by Amazon, this can be considered a secondary navigation system; however, it provides a direct link to specific sections of a website.

Site map: A single Web page which shows the complete navigation structure for your website. This is critical for SEO.

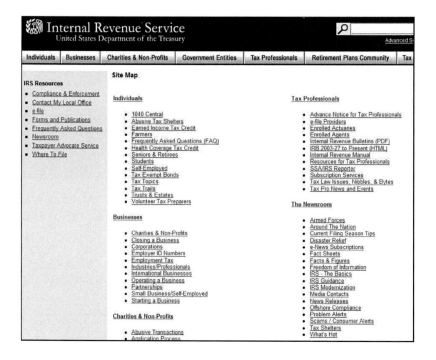

Drop-down menu: A menu, typically across the top or left hand side of a Web page that drops down or expands sub-menus as the mouse is moved over them. This lets you put many links into the navigation, but they stay collapsed except when used. These are typically made from JavaScript, DHTML, or CSS.

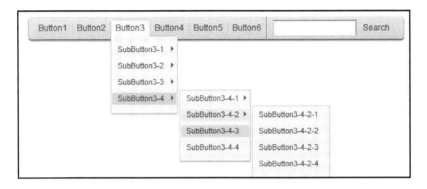

The bottom line is that simple, effective, user-friendly navigation is one of the most important elements of Web design. I recommend you spend some time visiting other sites to get an idea of how different navigation methods are used. This will not only give you great ideas for what to do, but it also helps you determine what to avoid.

Your navigation should be consistent throughout your blog. If you use buttons and drop down menus, they should appear on every page and in the same location. You should insert hyperlinks into your Web pages as another method; your visitors are familiar with hyperlinks and can easily recognize them when they're embedded into Web pages.

Make sure your navigation system is "above the fold." Above the fold is a term taken from the newspaper industry, which means the "important" stories are placed above the fold in a newspaper and less important stories are placed below the fold where they are not seen when viewing the front page. The concept translates to Web pages.

The following generic Web page image shows you how to successfully design your important content above the fold. The main banner is on the top third of the page, which would showcase the name and objective of your blog. To get to the posts, you can see that they are located in the middle of the page, which might warrant some slight scrolling, and to get to the other, less important information, the user must scroll to the bottom.

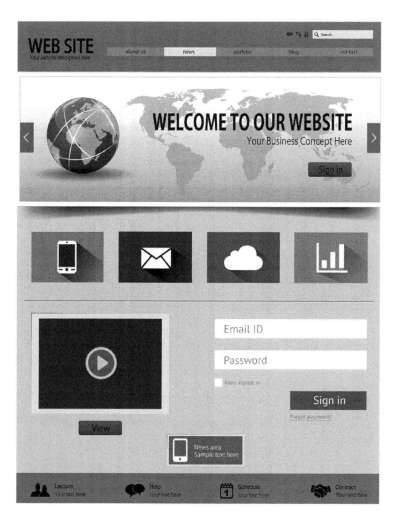

You only have so much real estate in a monitor, and you cannot always fit your entire page into the browser window. Make sure your navigation systems are above the fold on a Web page — they should never have to scroll to find your navigation system.

Make sure you have a "Home" navigation link on every page. Give your site visitors an easy way to get back to the home page.

Make your navigation systems attractive through the use of graphics, images, and advanced features such as a rollover button that changes color when a mouse is moved over the item.

Blog Must-Haves

Blogs can be simple or complex. However, there are some basic attributes every blog should have.

A home page

This is typically the first page a site visitor will see, and it is the anchor of your site. The focus of your design efforts should concentrate on your home page, and it should serve as the launch pad to other parts of your website. Some blogs may use a splash or entry page before you hit the home page; typically these are done in flash as an "intro" page, and they can be quickly by-passed to get the visitor to the main site content.

This page must have defined navigation which is easy to find and easy to use. You should have navigation links or navigation buttons, as well as excellent Web content that is keyword-rich and is easily read and understood by the blog visitor.

Search options

You have to have some form of search function on your blog. This can be done with a site map as well as through additional applets from Google and other companies, which will index your Web pages and give you free search capabilities.

I recommend using the Google Custom Search Engine, which you can get here: **https://cse.google.com/cse**; however, there are many others you can find with a quick Web search.

A privacy policy

Internet users are becoming increasingly concerned with their privacy. You should establish a "Privacy" Web page and let your visitors know exactly how you will be using the information you collect from them.

This page should address the following for your potential customers:

- For what purpose do you plan on using their information?

- Will their information be sold or shared with a third party?

- Why do you collect their email addresses?

- Do you track their IP addresses?

- Notify site visitors that you are not responsible for the privacy issues of any websites you may be linked to.

- Notify site visitors of your security measures in place to protect the misuse of their private or personal information.

- Provide site visitors with contact information in the event that they have any questions about your privacy statement.

An "about" page

An "About Us" page is an essential part of a professional website for a variety of reasons. Your potential customers may want to know exactly who you are, and it is a great opportunity to create a text-laden page for search engine visibility. An "About Us" page should include:

- A personal or professional biography of you
- A photograph of yourself
- A description of you
- Your mission
- Contact information, including an email address and social media links

A "feedback" page

There are many reasons to incorporate a feedback page into your blog. There are times when your followers will have comments or suggestions for you, and even if you end up disagreeing, it can still be very helpful. You can either do a separate feedback page, or you can just made a feedback widget where your followers can send in a comment.

Copyrighted material

You need to give credit to any and all material on your website that is not your own. A simple link with credit to the photographer and a short note about the license is usually enough, but check with the original author to see if they have any special preferences. Proper citation in accepted formats such as MLA is another one of the factors that search engines consider. This is one reason why Wikipedia® pages often get a high page rank.

Image leeching is considered bad manners in the world of Web development. Never use an image from another website without the expressed written permission of the website owner to make sure you're not violating any copyright laws. There have been instances where the original image owner replaced the images with "Don't Leech" signs. The signs can appear on the leecher's website without their knowledge, because the file link is still the same. This could create a tarnished reputation of the website in question, since hundreds of users might notice the signs before the site developer does.

Hosting images on your own server will take the element of risk and surprise away from all important content crucial to your website. You can find many free images online that are released under free and open licenses. Look for images marked "copyleft" or those released under the Creative Commons License. Be sure to read the license carefully to make sure you comply with the requirements listed before using the image for your website.

CHAPTER 5
FAMOUS TEEN BLOGGERS AND THEIR STORIES

I f you're reading all of this and are thinking — *okay, that's cool, but there's no way a blog that I start will amount to any-thing* — think again.

We have compiled a list of some of the youngest bloggers in the world, and they all have some pretty impressive success stories. Don't let your age stop you — if you have a passion for some-thing, the rest will follow.

Tavi Gevinson

Perhaps you've heard of her — Tavi is a young fashion icon known for starting a humble blog called "Style Rookie." She started the blog when she was 11 years old, but before she could think twice, her blog was seeing 30,000 visitors per day. One thing led to another, and she was invited to attend the New York Fashion Week and the Paris Fashion Week.

She started being featured in tons of famous magazines, she started her own t-shirt line, she spoke at a TED conference, and finally, she started her own magazine called "Rookie."

All of this from a start-up blog. Her first blog was full of photos of her eccentric outfits — she wasn't shy, and she took all of the photos from her backyard. People were drawn to her peculiar fashion sense, and her blog slowly started to reach more people.

Here is Tavi's first blog post:

"**Well I am new here**.... Lately I've been really interested in fashion, and I like to make binders and slideshows of "high-fashion" modeling and designs. I'd like to know of neat websites and magazines, so comments are welcome. I plan on posting pictures in the future, but for now, I'm just getting started. Yours truly, Tavi"

At 14 years old, she had silver hair, for example. Her style is cute, yet jarring. What sets her apart from the mainstream blogs is that she has such an unconventional, original style. Here is a short excerpt from a profile done by *The New Yorker (2010)*:

"Magazine editors envy her touch. Amy Astley, the editor of Teen Vogue, told me, 'Sometimes I say to my staff, *Wow, I had more fun reading the blog of this teenager than reading professional copy that we wrote.*'"

Her carefree edge sets her apart from everyone else; when you look at her blog, you get this overwhelming feeling of, *Wow, she really doesn't care what anyone else thinks.*

She's following her passions and isn't letting anyone get in her way.

She has been on Broadway, she's the new face of a Clinique ad campaign, and her net worth is well into the millions.

Nick Normile

At 15 years old, Nick started a culinary blog. He just wanted to post things about food, because that's what he was passionate about.

Here's an excerpt from Nick's first blog post:

"Hi, my name is Nick. As you may have guessed I'm 15, and a foodie, and an aspiring chef. [...] I plan to document my experiences at Lacroix, and to talk about everything else food related. Just remember, school comes first, and if I swear anywhere in this blog, don't tell my mom."

His blog ended up winning awards, and at one point, he was getting up to 10,000 hits in a single day. He was truly a successful teen blogger. In 2006, he was offered an apprenticeship at Lacroix at the Rittenhouse by the head chef Matthew Levin. After his apprenticeship, he worked at Amada, Osteria, and Fork. He has dined all over Philly (usually paid for by his allowance), and he was even featured in a story in the Philadelphia Inquirer (2007).

Food was really Nick's life — he read cookbooks before bed, he delighted (and kind of bewildered) his parents with extravagant dinners, and he saved up $250 to go to Per Se, famous chef Keller's Manhattan restaurant.

Nick has truly seen success, and the blogging world has noticed. But, something funny happened when I looked into Nick's blog. His last post was in 2012.

What happened?

Well, this is what he explains in one of his last posts:

> "Thinking on paper. First semester done. What now? I don't know what I'm doing. I miss the kitchen. Though I was able to do some cooking over break.
>
> Every now and then I feel like being Thomas Keller again. But I just don't know if the chef lifestyle is for me. Long shifts, low pay, physically exhausting work.
>
> [...] I don't know if I'd be able to pass up the opportunity to work in finance. Time will tell."

So, that's it. Nick went from being a budding star to ditching his famous blog, "Foodie at Fifteen" (**http://foodieatfifteen.blog spot.com**).

But, that's okay. He's young — you're young — and you're allowed to switch gears. If you're passionate about food now, but find that in five years you're ready for something else, then follow that instinct. You don't have to be interested in the same things forever.

But, once again, Nick shows us that passion brings success.

Zoella

If you're a beauty lover, you've probably heard of Zoe Elizabeth Sugg, the YouTube beauty queen.

Zoe created her blog (**www.zoella.co.uk**) and YouTube channel in 2009 at the age of 19 — by the end of the year, she had about 1,000 followers. As of 2016, she has 10.5 million.

Zoella's first blog post was created on February 18, 2009, and unlike Tavi and Nick, she jumps straight into it without any kind of introduction: "Okay, so for Valentines day, My boyfriend also bought me these two things from Lush.."

She goes on to post pictures of what she got as well as some detailed descriptions of what she thought of it all.

Her YouTube was basically an extension of her blog, with her first video being posted in December of 2009. It's titled "60 Things in My Bedroom." She shows things like gum, DVDs, a mirror, and her hair tools.

Her channel follows her life as a fashion and beauty enthusiast. She posts videos that showcase her favorite beauty products, her favorite outfits, and beauty hauls.

Zoella explains on her website that she's pinching herself at her insane success:

> "Before long, I had a small following of people that enjoyed reading what I'd written, and this was amazing in itself, as really, I'd never expected anyone to enjoy anything I'd written in my own little space on the Internet" (**www.zoella.co.uk/about-me**).

She emphasizes her passion — she was writing and blogging about things that she loved and never tired of. Before long, she signed a deal with Penguin and wrote two record-breaking books. Her debut book, "Online Girl," showcases what it's like to grow up in the digital age. Her Internet success has marked her as an influential icon, and she has even started her own makeup line called Zoella Beauty.

In 2011, Zoella won Cosmopolitan UK's "Best established beauty blog" award (VideoInk 2013). It only took her two years to get this place — you can do it, too.

Spencer Tweedy

Spencer Tweedy is a musician and photographer. He's also friends with Tavi. His dad is also a famous rock star (the leader of the band Wilco). So, you might not have a rock star for a dad, but Spencer's still a cool dude.

He wrote his first post in October of 2010, and it's a picture of a young boy, his eyes squeezed tightly shut, his cheeks pink from what we can only assume to be frosty air, his mouth slightly open, and his jaw clenched tight. The picture is labeled "Squint."

When you scroll through his older posts, you see that most of them are photographs that he's taken, from people to flowers to animals to doors. He has a way with lighting and angles, and all of them are strangely pleasant to look at.

His most recent posts center on his two bands, Tweedy and The Blisters.

Well, he's on tour now with his dad. He announced in March of 2016 that he's going to Australia, New Zealand, and Japan.

He's been featured on NPR and has written on Medium. His Medium post, "Tweedy Tour 2014 "reads: "This year, my dad and I began our first real tour together in support of Sukierae, the so-called 'solo album performed by a duo' we released in September. [...] I got to meet people who have been reading my writing since I was twelve years old."

His writing is what brought people to him, and while he may have gotten a big booster from his famous dad, he really did create a space of his own, particularly through his love of photography.

There's no doubt that Spencer loves what he does — check out his blog at **http://spencertweedy.com**.

Jeremy Salamon

Jeremy is also a chef, and he explains that his main goal is to connect with other food-lovers, which he has done by following his passion for cooking. He started writing about the dinner parties he cooked at, and he started getting noticed, particularly by AOL's KitchenDaily. They liked what they saw, and before he knew it, at 18 years old, Jeremy became the youngest contributor that AOL had ever contracted with.

The story really starts at nine years old, though, with Jeremy telling his parents that he would be a chef someday. He went from dreaming about it to scooping ice cream for the local country club to competing in culinary competitions.

Jeremy got where he is today solely because of his blog — he now attends the prestigious Culinary Institute of America (CIA) in Hyde Park, NY. He is also working on his first book as well as "some very exciting new projects."

This is exciting news for you — if you love something, just start writing about it. It can't hurt, right? You see how clearly Jeremy's writing spiraled into awesome opportunities (I mean, he's writing a book).

Here is an excerpt from Jeremy's first blog post from May of 2009:

"Ok, so I know its way past mothers day but I just had to tell you of my frozen truffle experience. I always make my mom something on Mothers Day (her favorite is Linzer Tart Cookies) but this Mothers Day I wanted to make something different."

He has come a super long way, and he loves what he does. He's graduated from his blog to bigger things, but without that platform, who knows where he'd be?

You can check out his blog at **http://jeremycooks.com**.

Calur Villade

Calur Villade, which is a stage name (her real name is Paolina Russo), is very into fashion and visual art. When you scroll through her blog, you're taken aback by all the strange images — clashing colors, abstract art, hot pink hair, her foot in the shower... it's strange, yet artsy.

She started her blog at 14, and here is her first post, titled "Just Do It" (2010):

"No, I am no endorser of nike, but I have been thinking lately. I really want to start a blog. For a month now, I have been planning. Planning on what I should write in my first post. How I should look. My name. What font. What picture. Planning on what the overall message

I would portray to the people who read it. I wanted things to be PERFECT. And that just killed me. [...]

lame story, I know. But well I'm new to this whole blogging thing and it's all just a shot in the dark. I have no clue as to what I am doing. We will see what happens. Go with the flow? and if you are wondering what the heck my blog name means, and what language it is, long story short I LOVE (with all my heart) VALUE VILLAGE. Let's just leave it at that. Cheers to my first post! (and by cheers, we are clinking glasses of lemonade, not alcohol)

Paolina"

She posts pictures of fashion designs she loves as well as overall inspirational posts.

She has been featured on other fashion blogs such as Rookie (Tavi sure seems to be everywhere, doesn't she?). She continues to blog about things she loves and is passionate about, and she's grabbing everyone's attention. She was featured on Guest of a Guest's site in the article "Teen Dream: The Top Bloggers Under 18."

She can really only go up from here.

Monik Pamecha

At 13 years of age, Monik started the blog Etiole, a technology-based blog. The "About" section of the blog explains that this blog is awesome because all of the writers are under 13 years old.

You might be thinking — what the heck are 13 years old going to be able to teach me?

Well, here are some examples of posts:

- "Why The iPhone 5c Won't Sell More Than The 5s"

- "Bose Introduces Some New Audio Gear: QuietComfort 20 and the SoundLink Mini"

- "Is HR Using Facebook in the Hiring Process?"

- "How to Find a Song Name by Lyrics, Humming, Beats or Melody"

When you scroll through the blog, you're bound to be intrigued by at least a post or two. Monik does write a lot of the posts, but he has guest writers who contribute as well. He has a pretty extensive "Write for Us" page where he explains the submission process.

He even has an "Advertise" page where he lets you know how to advertise on his blog! In case you were wondering, he obviously has a privacy policy, too.

Monik's blog is very sophisticated, and he has a pretty substantial reader base — in 2009, The Economic Times reported that Monik's blog had 16,000 subscribers.

In 2013, the University of Pennsylvania wrote an article about Monik and explained that he sees between 50,000 and 80,000 unique monthly visitors. His own posts have earned him about $2,000. We can only imagine what that has skyrocketed to now.

Monik is focused on regularly posting to his blog as well as expanding it. Keep your eye out — he's the one to watch.

CHAPTER 6
HOW TO MAKE MONEY

Y ou're following your passion by turning it into a blog — you're already halfway there to becoming successful in the moneymaking department. So, how can you monetize your blog? This chapter will teach you everything you need to know to turn your blog posts into cash.

Advertising with Google AdSense

Google AdSense lets you place Google advertisements on your blog, which earns money for each click by site visitors. You make money when people click on an ad, and you don't have to do anything but host the ad on your site.

You do need to recognize that money you make from ads is merely supplemental income of an unknown amount, which you are trading off for hosting advertisements on your site or blog. In other words, you probably won't be able to buy that Lamborghini just by hosting ads on your blog.

> ☞ *Fast Fact:*
>
> If your click through rate (CTR) is 1%, and your cost per click (CPC) is 25 cents, then you need 100,000 visitors a day to make $100,000 a year from Google AdSense (Mohan 2016).

Google puts relevant CPC (cost-per-click) and CPM (cost per thousand impressions) ads through the same auction and lets them compete against one another. The auction for the advertisement takes place instantaneously, and Google AdSense subsequently displays a text or image ad(s) that will generate the maximum revenue for you.

Becoming an AdSense publisher is very simple. You can fill out a brief application form online at **www.google.com/AdSense**, which requires your website to be reviewed before your application is approved. Once approved, Google will email you HTML code to place on your Web pages. Once the HTML code is saved onto your Web page, it activates, and targeted ads will be displayed on your website.

You can also make money by putting a Google search box on your website, which literally pays you for search results. This service may help keep traffic on your site longer since site visitors can search directly from your site. This is free for you to do, and it's super simple — why not?

Google says that their "ad review process ensures that the ads you serve are not only family-friendly, but also comply with our strict editorial guidelines. We combine sensitive language filters, your input, and a team of linguists with good hard common sense to automatically filter out ads that may be inappropriate for your content." You don't have to worry about inappropriate content on your blog is basically what that means.

You can customize the appearance of your ads, choosing from a wide range of colors and templates. This is also the case with Google's search results page. To track how much money you make, Google has a ton of tools you can use.

Setting Up Your Campaign

Once you fill out the application form, it's pretty important that you at least browse through the terms of service. In particular, you must agree that you won't tamper with the ads on your page.

In other words, you can't click on your ads, have others click on your ads, or place text on your website asking anyone to click on your ads. The reason for this is simple — Google doesn't want you to generate revenue by clicking on your own ads (it's like stealing).

Welcome to AdSense What is AdSense? | Already have an account?
Please complete the application form below.

Website Information

Website URL: [?]	
	• Please list your primary URL only. • Example: www.example.com
Website language:	Select a language ▼
	• Tell us your website's primary language to help our review process

Contact Information

Account type: [?]	Select an account type ▼
Country or territory:	Select a country or territory ▼

Important - Your payment will be sent to the address below. Please complete all fields that apply to your address, such as a full name, full street name and house or apartment number, and accurate country, ZIP code, and city. Example.

Payee name (full name):	
	• Checks will be made out to this name and mailed to the address below. • Payee must be at least 18 years of age to participate in AdSense. • No initials in the name - learn more
Address line 1:	
Address line 2 (optional):	
City:	
State, province or region:	
Zip or postal code:	
Country or territory:	Select a country or territory
	• To change your country or territory, please change your selection at the top of this form.
Phone:	
Fax (optional):	
Email preference:	We'll send you service announcements that relate to your agreement with Google. ☑ In addition, send me periodic newsletters with tips and best practices and occasional surveys to help Google improve AdSense.

Product Selection

Product(s): [?]	☑ AdSense for Content ☑ AdSense for Search

Policies

AdSense applicants must agree to adhere to AdSense program policies (details)	☐ I agree that I will not click on the Google ads I'm serving through AdSense. ☐ I will not place ads on sites that include incentives to click on ads. ☐ I agree that I can receive checks made out to the payee name I have listed above. ☐ I will not place ads on sites that include pornographic content. ☐ I certify that I have read the AdSense Program Policies.

Screenshots © Google Inc. and are reproduced with permission.

When your website is reviewed and your account is approved, you will receive a confirmation email.

To quickly set up your account, follow these steps:

Step 1) Log in to your account.

Step 2) Create and apply your AdSense code. This can sound confusing, but we promise it isn't. Click on the "AdSense Setup" tab and follow the guided steps to create your code. Then, copy that code and paste it into the HTML source of your site.

If you don't know how to add the HTML code to your blog, visit **https://support.google.com/adsense/answer/181947?hl=en &ref_topic=28893&rd=1**. If you don't want to type out that long address, you can just as easily do a Web search with keywords like "How to Implement Google AdSense Code."

Step 3) Watch the money flow in! After your ads start, you can see how much you've made at any time by checking the "Reports" tab in your account.

> ☞ *Fast Fact:*
>
> Some of the top paying AdSense niches are finance, internet marketing, technology, web hosting, internet & computers, software, and health. Some of the lowest paying AdSense niches are entertainment, arts, movies, celebrity gossips, news blogs, jokes, wallpapers, quotes, recipes, and photo blogs (Mohan 2016).

Reviewing for Money

This is a very controversial subject, but it has definitely gained some popularity. In short, companies will pay you (the blogger) to do what you do best — blog. The catch is that you must write about whatever product, service, website, or company that you're asked to blog about in a very nice way. You're basically getting paid to give a positive review.

Do your blog posts truly reflect your "real" opinions? In this type of set-up, they may or may not. Often times, a company will have you sign a contract saying that you'll leave a positive review before they even send you the product in the first place.

Respected bloggers can lose credibility when they blog for cash. The true purpose of blogging is open communication and opinions; these too are often lost in the quest for cash. To be fair, most pay-for-blogging services state that you pick what you want to blog on and are free to post whatever you want about the topic (within the terms of service), and some require disclosure. Disclosure simply means that your blog posts will reveal to others that you are getting paid for the blog post — "this company sponsored this post."

Here are four of the top pay-for-blogging sites:

PayPerPost (PPP): This is a site that helps connect you with advertisers that want to sponsor specific content. In a nutshell, you search through a list of "Opportunities," you make a post, you get your content approved, and you get paid. It's as easy as that. You can earn as much as $20 for a blog post, and PayPerPost does require disclosure.

Blogvertise: Blogvertise pretty much does the same thing as PPP. This site wants you to talk about specific websites, products, or services on your blog. In exchange, you get paid through PayPal. The advertisers on this site actually get to choose from a pool of bloggers, and then you are told which products or services you're supposed to write about. You can make between $4-$25 per post. Your blog is required to be at least 60 to 100 words, and it must contain a minimum of three or more links. Endorsing the website product or service is not a requirement.

ReviewMe: Reviewme.com is almost a combination of the previous two services. This lets advertisers create campaigns that bloggers may choose to review. These advertisers also have the option to choose which blogger reviews their campaign, but it costs more. You can make between $20-$200 for each review. You must submit an application and get accepted to be eligible as a participating blogger.

CREAMaid: You create a CREAMaid conversation widget and insert it into your blog post. Your post is now eligible to be "selected." Once selected, it is syndicated to all participating posts throughout the network and you receive a payment. In essence, advertisers will create a "conversation widget." The conversation widget tells you what topic to write about. You must accept it and write about the topic in a post. If the advertiser selects your post, it's incorporated in participating blogs across the network.

One key factor with making this kind of money is that you must qualify. While qualification terms vary, most require you to have a well-established, quality blog with significant posts (i.e., you need to be a very established and reputable blogger for your opinion to be of value). Do some research, and you will find that there are dozens of other pay-for-blogging websites, all with differing terms and conditions.

Become an Affiliate

Another way to make money through your blog is to become an affiliate. What this means is that you promote a certain product, and if someone buys it, you get a certain percentage of it.

There are several companies that do this kind of thing.

Amazon Associates

This program allows you to choose from millions of products to advertise them to your subscribers. They have various methods of linking — you can link directly to your blog, you can share the link on social media, you can link to a specific product and build customized text links, you can create a banner, or you can create an online store.

For example, I've seen many health and fitness bloggers create their own Amazon store within their blog. They'll have a recipe with some hard-to-find ingredients, and they'll have a "Buy these ingredients here" link. That will take you to their Amazon store. If you end up buying any of the products, they get a small commission from Amazon.

Amazon pays you different amounts depending on what it is that you're advertising. It's generally a pretty small percentage, but every little bit helps, right? Here are some examples:

- Grocery products get you 4%
- DVDs gct you 4%
- Game downloads get you 10%
- Electronics get you 4%
- Headphones get you 6%

It doesn't require too much effort from you to make some money off of this program — all you have to do is sign up. Here's where you can do it: **https://affiliate-program.amazon.com**.

LinkShare

When you visit the site (the name bounces between LinkShare and Rakuten Affiliate Network — they are the same thing), you are asked if you want to be a publisher (this would be you, the blogger wanting to make money) or an advertiser (this would be the person wanting to promote their product). The site was voted the #1 Affiliate Marketing Network for five years in a row.

It's just like any other affiliate program in that you make commission directly from your blog. However, the site does make it clear that they want someone with a "loyal following." The advertisers don't want to pay commission to be on a blog with no subscribers — we don't blame them. The only not-cool part about that is that if you are just starting your blog, you can't really make money from this program.

However, once you have a decent amount of posts and have been able to get some followers, you might be ready for this step.

If you decide to join, you have to sign up. The site asks you for your company information, your contact and account information, your website information, and your payment threshold.

If you aren't ready to sign up and just want to start a conversation, you can fill out their contact form, which asks you for your contact information, your business details like revenue and site visitors, and your overall interests. Do so here: **http://marketing. rakuten.com/lets-talk**.

There's no harm in applying — just remember that if you don't have a daily following, you should wait or else the big brands won't be interested in you as an affiliate.

Commission Junction (CJ) Affiliate

You can be an advertiser or publisher on this site, as well. CJ Affiliate helps you make commissions, but what sets them apart is that they have the most well-known brands. They boast about having more Internet Retailer Top 500 advertisers than any other network, and they also say that they pay the best.

Their site is very sophisticated with easy-to-use tools like a Publisher Toolbox, a Deep Link Generator, Widgets, and Tracking tools. They make the whole process extremely painless.

The site has some recommendations for you in order to make sure advertisers accept your application. Here are some of them:

- Be committed
  - o Optimize your site
  - o Have quality content
  - o Have a great design
  - o Have time to commit
- Have a game plan
  - o Maintain and update your site regularly
  - o Build traffic
  - o Be unique
  - o Have engaging content

- Be different
  - o   Have a professional site
  - o   Get quality subscribers
  - o   Complete an action
  - o   Commit to the future

Long story short, CJ wants to make sure that your blog is solid before jumping in. If it isn't, you could end up with some fees — if your blog doesn't generate any "commissionable" transactions for a period of six months, your account will be deactivated, and a non-refundable $10 fee will be handed to you.

If you think you're ready for this big step, sign up here: **www.cj.com/publisher-sign**.

EBay Partner Network

Last, but certainly not least (there are tons of affiliate programs on the Web), is the eBay Partner Network. The site explains that eBay has everything — whatever you're looking to promote, you'll be able to find it. They also have user-friendly tools as well as an active community that can help you if you get stuck.

Like Amazon, eBay gives you a small percentage of the item, and that percentage varies depending on the category. EBay has a list of the percentages you earn, but remember that it's based off of the revenue that eBay makes — not the cost of the item itself. Here are some examples:

- Fashion gets you 65% of the profit
- Electronics get you 55% of the profit
- Vehicles get you 50% of the profit
- Parts and Accessories get you 70% of the profit

They also pay you every month, so you can expect a steady payment. When you first sign up, they give you a commission bonus for the first three months, which pretty much triples the percentages you see above. You can sign up here: **https://partner network.ebay.com**.

They do mention that you should have a successful platform. They explain it by saying you might be "a person with a popular Twitter feed, a blogger with a growing following or an owner of a successful website."

So, like most of the other options, you should wait to start making money through affiliate programs until you actually have people to market the products to.

4 Affiliate Marketing Myths (Forbes 2014)

1. These programs are quick and easy to use

2. You must work in a very popular niche

3. Affiliate marketing is an outdated strategy

4. The more sites you're on, the better

Use Your Blog as a Platform

In the end, you might not make a ton of money off of traditional advertising techniques, reviewing, or affiliate marketing. The bottom line is: if you don't have a big subscriber base, you won't be able to make that much money. The thing about blogging is that you now have an online platform that you can use to do bigger and better things (like writing books, selling products or services, or creating courses).

BEST SELLER
Chapter One

In other words, you can use your blog as a springboard to sell things. Here are some examples:

Leo Babauta, creator of the website Zen Habits

He used his platform to write and sell several books, to teach mindfulness courses, to develop an app, and to create a habit mastery program. Visit his site here: **http://zenhabits.net**.

He explains how he makes money from his website, and he actually has a "no copyright" policy, which means that you can share and use his work anywhere without legal trouble. Here's a very helpful article from his site — he has some really valuable things to say about making money on the Internet, so read up.

HOW I CONDUCT MY BUSINESS

By Leo Babauta

Through trial and error, I learned some principles that work for me. I don't share them here to show that I'm superior to anyone, but to show an example of what might work for you. To show that doing things that feel right can make a business succeed.

Here's how I conduct my business.

1. **Readers first.** This is my No. 1 rule, and it has served me extremely well. When I have a question ("should I promote X or not?") the answer is always, "What would my readers want? What would help them most?" When the choice is between making some extra money or my readers' interest, the choice is obvious. There is no choice. I can't tell you how many times I've passed up being part of a mega-sale or affiliate marketing campaign that would have earned me $50K (and sometimes much more) in a day or two if I'd decided to participate. I've walked away from at least $1M because it would have put profits before my readers. And I think my readers trust me more because of this (see next item).

2. **Trust is everything.** The most valuable assets I have are my readers' trust and attention. And the attention will go really fast if they stop trusting me. Everything else in this list is based around these first two principles. When you start doing affiliate marketing, even if you think it would help the reader, if it would make them question your motives (is he trying to help me or make some money here?), it erodes their trust, a little at a time. That's not worth the money.

3. **Make money by helping.** I put out products and courses that I think will really help people, and that's how I make money. This works really well for me. People are happy because their lives are better, and I'm happy because the revenue I make is entirely coming from making people's lives better. We both win, our lives are all enriched. This is not the case from advertising (see next item).

4. **No ads, affiliate marketing.** These are both the same, really. When you market someone else's product as an affiliate, it's just a hidden form of advertising. I should note that I had ads and did affiliate marketing for a couple years before giving it up. Why'd I give it up? Well, I realized (through experimentation) that the return on this kind of business model is very bad. You get very little revenue, and erode trust. That's a bad formula for making money. When you sell an ad, what you're really selling is your readers' attention and trust — they trust you to put something important in front of their attention, and you capitalize on that. Of course, most readers learn *not* to trust the ads, and try to skip them, and put up with them because they want the good content (or service) you're giving them. So they no longer trust you as much, but put up with your revenue tactics. This sucks. Who wants their customers to *put up* with anything? Why not delight them with how you make money? Why not enrich them? Now, can everyone do this? Possibly not, but I wouldn't reject the idea without giving it a genuine shot.

5. **Just the text** – no social media buttons, popups, dropdowns, or anything else that annoys or distracts. This goes back to trust — people come to my site to read something that will add value to their lives. Not to be pushed to share something on social media, or like something, or subscribe to my email newsletter. Yes, I have a thing at the bottom to subscribe, but it's not pushy, and I don't promise any gimmicky downloads. When your site has a popup or dropdown that asks people to subscribe, it's annoying. I'm sorry to be blunt but I'm speaking as a reader now — I will never go back to a site that does that. Which means I don't read a lot of my friends' sites because they do this. Give the readers what they want, and nothing else, and you won't have to ask them to subscribe or share. They'll do it on their own, and this is the kind of share and subscriber you want.

6. **Uncopyright.** My site has been uncopryrighted since January 2008 (there weren't any other sites doing this at the time), and in the last 5+ years, uncopyright has not only *not* hurt my business, I strongly believe it's helped tremendously. Why? Because it helps people share and spread my work much more easily. If someone wants to use an article of mine, they don't have to go through the

hassle of trying to contact me and ask permission — they just use it. This has caused people to use my work in books, magazines, blogs, newsletters, classroom materials, art, conferences and more. This is amazing. In addition, uncopyright promotes the idea of sharing, and when you share with people, they tend to trust you more. Sharing builds trust.

7. **No sales.** I've seen many people do three-day sales of their products (or something similar), but I've never done one of these (that I can recall). Why not? Because it makes no sense to the reader (remember, readers first). Tell me the reader: why are you lowering the price of your product for three days? Why only those three days? If you can lower the price for those days, why not the other days? Is it to make more money from me (manipulate me into buying the book)? Is the price too high on the other days? What if I already bought the book at the higher price — was I ripped off? These are questions the reader has no answers to, and no matter how much you try to justify the reasons of the sale, it doesn't make sense. Either set the price at the higher price point (because you think it's worth it), or set it at the lower price point (because you want to get it into the hands of more people).

8. **Admit mistakes.** It might sound like I'm pretending to be perfect at what I do, but the truth is I'm winging it. I'm making it up as a I go along, in hopes that I won't screw it up, and constant fear that I am badly messing up. I have more trust in this process (and in my readers) now that I've been doing it for seven years and nothing has fallen apart, but I have made many mistakes along the way. I've been overly promotional, I've done affiliate marketing (just a couple of times), I had advertising, I asked people to share my work, I asked for votes. Those were mistakes, but I learned from them and try my best not to repeat them. Recently, in my Sea Change Program, I removed old habit modules from 2013 (I felt they were outdated), and my members were upset. I fixed the mistake and put the modules back. People don't expect you to be perfect — they do expect you to try your best to fix mistakes when you make them. I admit my mistakes, and try to rectify them and do better. People trust me more because of it, I think.

9. **Don't front.** I don't pretend I'm more than I am. I think there's a tendency in the online world to overrepresent yourself — put yourself off as an expert or the world's leading whateverthehell. But I'm not the world's leading anything. I am just a guy who has a wife and six kids, who has changed his life by making small habit changes, one at a time. A guy who has simplified his life and focused on being mindful. I've learned a lot from these experiences, and share them as much as I can here on Zen Habits. That's all I am, and I don't try to be more. When you only try to be yourself, you can't fail.

10. **Forget about stats, focus on helping.** In the early days, I was obsessed about site statistics. I would check my stats counter several times a day, look at where all the traffic was coming from, try to get my numbers up. Here's the thing: you can't do anything with those stats. If you're getting traffic from Reddit or Twitter, you can't do anything about that. All you can do, once you've seen the stats, is try to create great content. Try to help people. Try to add value. That's what you'd do even if you had zero stats. The stats don't change what you should do — though they might motivate you to do things you shouldn't do to get the stats up, things that aren't trustworthy. The stats just make you obsessive. About three years ago, I removed all stats trackers from my site, and now am freed from that worry. Now I focus on what really matters: helping people as best I can.

11. **Do what feels right.** This is vague and isn't very helpful at first, because in the beginning, you're never really sure what's "right". There are lots of choices to make and it always seems smart to just do what other people are doing, what the experts tell you to do. Unfortunately, that's often wrong. Everyone else does what everyone else does because that seems safer, and so they act out of fear of doing the wrong thing. In fact, safer is not the right thing. Doing the right thing is going to be against the mainstream. For example, when I gave up copyright, or let go of ads or social media buttons or affiliate marketing, or comments, those were all very scary things for me. It was against what everyone else at the time was doing. But in the end, I knew they were the right thing, because it was what was best for my readers. And it made me

> feel good about what I was doing. This is the compass you need to develop, to build trust with your readers, and with yourself. Feel good about what you're doing, don't act out of fear.

Gretchen Rubin, creator of the blog Gretchen Rubin

Yeah, that title is kind of lame, but her blog is called Gretchen Rubin (**www.gretchenrubin.com**). She focuses on creating happiness and developing good habits. That's what she writes about, and that's how she makes her living. Through her blog, she was able to write several books that have landed on the *New York Times* Bestseller list: "Better Than Before," "The Happiness Project," and "Happier at Home."

She also has a weekly podcast that hit #6 on iTunes the first day it launched. It ranks in the top 1% of podcasts and was named in iTunes's and Vulture's lists of "Best Podcasts of 2015." Her mission is to change lives by helping people move toward happiness and better habits. People flock to her, and she's been able to make a really great living by using her site as a way to promote herself.

Lori Deschene, Tiny Buddha Founder

Lori is the founder of Tiny Buddha (**http://tinybuddha.com**), which actually started on Twitter as a "quote of the day" account. Now, her Twitter account has almost 500,000 followers, and her blog has about one million monthly readers.

Her site is all about providing inspiration for people, and she was able to turn that online presence into a book, called "Tiny Buddha, Simple Wisdom for Life's Hard Questions ." She now has several books, products, and courses, and her online presence is only growing.

In the end, it can be difficult to make money if you don't have a lot of page views. If you want to get serious about blogging, you're going to have to take a step into the world of blog promoting. The next chapter will break it down and make it easy for you to get your name out there. But, first! Here's a quick tip and some advice from an expert.

> ☞ *Quick Tip:*
>
> Check out Amy Lynn Andrew's blog post about how to make money from your blog — she has a lot of interesting and unique ideas: **https://amylynnandrews.com/how-to-make-money-blogging**.

FROM THE EXPERTS: ELISE BAUER

Find her at:
www.simplyrecipes.com.

Why is marketing to bloggers a good idea? Inbound links from blogs improves Google rank, which increases traffic from search engines. Exposure from bloggers can land a company's website on a social bookmarking site, driving thousands of new visitors to the site. Bloggers are perceived to be more "authentic" than traditional media, making them disproportionately influential given their size. They can also be highly targeted, engaging the very audience that a marketer might want to reach. But bloggers are a more fickle bunch than most traditional media people. Marketing to them appropriately can yield great results; approaching them the wrong way can backfire.

As someone with a well-trafficked blog and a high Google rank, I get bombarded with marketing requests every day.

"Your site would be great for my SEO, would you please link to it?"

"You obviously love food. I would love to send you some of my ice cream for dogs and you could write about it if you wanted to." (Both real examples.)

Most pitches receive a cursory glance and get deleted without a second thought. A few get a response from me, especially if the pitch is respectful and polite. Even fewer get the response the marketer was hoping for. So, what's the trick?

If you are considering reaching out to bloggers, here are a few guidelines that may help you be more effective in your approach. Note that marketing to bloggers is sort of like selling vacuums door-to-door in a neighborhood where almost everyone knows each other, and most are chatting with each other over their fences. In any strong blogging community there is a lot of back-channel talk going on. This can work to your advantage or disadvantage, depending on how you approach the bloggers in the first place. Now for the guidelines — let's start with the "Don'ts."

Marketing to Bloggers Don'ts

Do not send obvious form letters. Did you know that we bloggers share the form letters we receive from marketers with each other? We do. This is a great way to get nowhere with the very people you are trying to influence. It also demonstrates that you have done practically no research whatsoever on your audience. Form letters result in promoting pork sausages to vegans or pitches for ready-to-eat cheesecake filling to gourmet scratch cooks.

Do not ask for links, unless you are willing to pay for them, at which point the conversation turns to advertising policy and rates. This whole reciprocal link thing might be barely tolerable on a blogger-to-blogger level, but is considered annoying spam when it comes from a company pushing products.

Do not leave blog comments plugging your products. Talk about generating ill will! It's called blog spam. As a blogger I don't really care that you think my readers would be interested in your ready-made lemon syrup. I'm not interested in allowing a company to promote its products on my blog without my permission. If you abuse comments, eventually you'll generate such bad feelings that people will start writing in their blogs about how your company is spamming the blogosphere. Then the next time someone looks your company up in Google all they'll see is a litany of complaints. Not exactly the intended result, eh?

Do not come on too strong. If you send out product, you can follow up with a "did you receive it?" but not a "when are you going to write about it?" Do not insist on anything. And if people don't want to promote your product, please don't argue with them. Thank them for their time and move on.

Do not put the blogger on your mailing list (unless they have requested it). This should be obvious, shouldn't it? But clearly it isn't, as getting put on some random marketer's email newsletter or mailing list happens all the time. Bloggers hate it.

Marketing to Bloggers Do's

Start by creating a targeted list of bloggers. Use tools such as Technorati, BlogPulse, or Alexa to help find blogs that speak to your target audience. Note that although the biggest blogs may be more influential, they tend to get hit up all the time for marketing requests and may not be that responsive. So don't ignore a blog just because it has 20 inbound links (as accounted for by Technorati) and not 200. It may be just the blog you want.

Know the blogs you are approaching. Before you email a blogger with a pitch, read through the last two months of their posts. Really. At least that. Understand what they care about, what they write about. You'll get a much better feel for how your pitch will be received if you know who it is you are pitching to. Learn the name and gender of the blogger; it may not be immediately obvious. Address the blogger by name instead of just "Hello" or "Dear Webmaster." Check to see if the blogger has posted a review policy. Many bloggers simply will not do product reviews; you risk annoying them if they have a published policy that you have ignored.

Treat the blogger with the same respect you would a professional journalist. It's good manners. Many bloggers have a lot more influence than you would imagine, yet they are often treated as if they are inconsequential. If you treat them well, you will be rewarded in kind.

Be open to constructive feedback. If you send out a pitch and it's off the mark, most likely you will get more than a few angry emails back. If you are lucky, someone will take the time to offer polite, constructive feedback as to how you could reach out to bloggers more effectively. Listen to this advice. Consider it valuable consulting that you would normally have to pay thousands of dollars for and here this very nice blogger is giving it to you for free. Treat that blogger well. Assume you know nothing about marketing to bloggers, because believe me, unless you are a blogger who gets pitched all the time, you don't.

Offer to send product, no strings attached. If you have a book you're promoting, offer to send it to the blogger. Don't suggest that the blogger write a review. If she likes it enough, she might. Or she might recommend it to another blogger who ends up writing about it. Don't underestimate the social power of reciprocity. By giving a gift, if the receiver likes it, he'll likely find ways to make it up to you. This is also why some bloggers don't accept gifts or promotional product. They don't want to be indebted to anyone. So, if a blogger says no, don't take it personally.

At the end of the day, it all comes down to the Golden Rule: Treat bloggers the way you would like to be treated yourself. Unlike you, the marketing professional, who probably gets paid to reach out to them, most bloggers do what they do purely for the joy of personal self-expression. They pour hundreds, if not thousands of hours of their lives into their personal blogging outpost. Respect that and you might get somewhere with them.

Elise Bauer has advised technology companies on their business and marketing strategies for over 20 years. Elise's clients have included Apple Computer,

Symantec, Warner Music Group, Creative Labs, and a host of technology start-up companies. Elise received her MBA and BS degrees from Stanford University. In 2003, Elise created the award winning Simply Recipes (www.simplyrecipes.com), a food and cooking blog, which has grown to reach over 40,000 visitors a day, and produces more than three million page views per month. In February of 2007, Elise was named by the Wall Street Journal as one of the "hidden influencers" of the Web. You can find Pacifica Group online at **www.pacifica-group.com**.

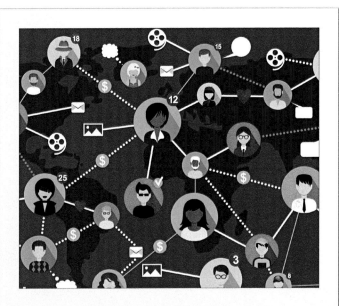

CHAPTER 7
GETTING MORE
SUBSCRIBERS (FOR FREE!)

Y ou're ready for the next step — blog promotion. You don't have to have a business degree to master this, either. There are tons of free ways to promote your blog. You don't have to spend money to be successful — if you're passionate and Internet-savvy, you can end up like any of the famous bloggers we talked about in Chapter 5.

Here are tons of ways you can get more subscribers without spending a dime.

Placement of Your URL

Sometimes it's all about where you link to your blog URL. Place your blog URL on your email signature so that every time you send an email, people can see your blog. You might get some clicks out of that.

It's also important to put a link to your blog on all of your social media accounts — Facebook, Twitter, Instagram — link to your blog everywhere. Seriously, everywhere.

Write Articles

Write articles and submit them to professional e-zines, article directories, and others to publish. Be sure to include a release allowing your article to be reprinted or redistributed, but only with proper attribution to you (at a minimum, include your name, email, and blog URL).

Use the Internet

Use a free pinging service to hit all the major search engines. It's pretty quick and simple to do. I recommend **http://pingomatic. com** and **http://feedshark.brainbliss.com**.

You can also submit your blog to directory services. A good list is available online at **www.toprankblog.com/rss-blog-directories**.

**FROM THE EXPERTS:
GREGORY A. WHITE**

1. Submit your blog to all of the directories listed on **http://pingo matic.com**. Pingomatic will ping 15 services all at once.

2. Ping your blog after every post at http://pingomatic.com.

3. Here's a real gem: Submit your blog to **http://www.pingoat.com**. Pingoat will ping over 50 blog ping services all at once. So you don't have to hunt for ping services and manually ping them. Pingoat pings over 50 blog ping servers (growing) with just one click.

4. Ping your blog after every post at Pingoat at **http://www.ping oat.com**.

5. Sign up for a free account at **BlogExplosion.com** and register your blog there.

6. Submit your blog to all of the directories listed at **www.rss-feeds-directory.com/blog_lists.html**. (Use **http://top200-blog-rss-submit.com** to simplify the process.)

7. Sign up for a "My Yahoo" at **http://my.yahoo.com** and attach your blog to your own "My Yahoo" account. This will get your blog included in Yahoo very quickly. This is worth the effort to stop what you're doing right now and do it, since Yahoo has a PR 9.

8. Use this code: "**http://add.my.yahoo.com/content?url= http://www.yourblog.com/urblog.xml**" in your blog to allow others to put your feed on their own "My Yahoo" account.

9. Sign up for a "My MSN" at **www.my.msn.com**, and attach your blog to your own "My MSN" account. This will get your blog included in MSN very quickly. This is also invaluable because MSN has a PR 8.

10. Use this code: "**http://my.msn.com/addtomymsn.armx?id=rss& ut=http://www.urblogfeedaddress.com/urblog.xml**" in your blog to allow others to put your feed on their own "My MSN" account.

11. Place the link and description of your blog in your signature, so that any posts to Forums, Outgoing Emails, Autoresponder Courses, etc., will promote your blog.

12. Post a link and description of your blog on each of your sites.

13. Place your blog on all the major search engines. **AddMe.com** will submit your blog free to the top 14 search engines here: **www.addme.com/submission.htm**. SubmitExpress.com will submit your blog free to the top 20 Search engines here: **www.submitexpress.com**.

14. Use Article Directories as a resource for articles to post on your blog. Here are a few:

    - **http://ezinearticles.com**
    - **http://goarticles.com**
    - **www.knowledge-finder.com**
    - **www.informit.com/articles**

15. Locate blogs with a lot of traffic and place useful comments in their comment box. Be sure the blog and your comments are relevant to both your blog and theirs. Senseless posts won't help you; they'll hurt you.

16. Once you get around five to ten posts on your blog, start a PR campaign and announce it to all relevant channels.

17. Make a blog post as often as possible. More than once a day is not really necessary. Remember, if you can't write that much, go to step # 14.

Greg White, Internet Marketer, Author, Consultant and Project Manager has been running successful Web projects since 2001. His sites and blogs cover Blog Marketing Tactics, Internet Marketing Tactics and a variety of 'Niche' topics, in addition to starting and marketing profitable Web projects.

Find him at **www.blogmarketingtactics.com** *and* **http://socialbuzzmaster.com.**

Navbar for Blogger

Take a look at the Navbar if you are using Blogger. This is the non-intrusive replacement for advertisements on Blogger. You may not even notice the Navbar (across the top of the screen on Blogger hosted blogs), but there is a button called "Next Blog" where users can click and be served a random blog. There are lots of people who find this as a good way to pass time. Your blog will be pulled in automatically.

If you're using Blogger, ensure you allow your blog to be added to the Blogger listing. To get some assistance when it comes to helping people find your blog, visit **https://support.google.com/blogger/answer/41373**.

Be an Active Blogger

When you're a really active blogger, people notice. If you're always commenting on other people's blogs, following them, and liking their posts, they might take a look at your page, and they might (just might!) follow you and return the favor. This is one of the ways to get your name out there — just be sure to have a quick and easy link back to your blog if you do comment on someone's post. Not only will the blogger notice, but other commenters might take a peak at your blog, too.

Feedburner

Sign up for a free Feedburner account (**www.feedburner.com**), and use it to promote your blog.

Linking

Offer to exchange links with other websites and blogs. All you have to do is send them an email that goes a little like this: "I love your content, and I think you'd like mine, too. Would you be interested in doing a cross-link with me? It could be a great promotional tool for both of us."

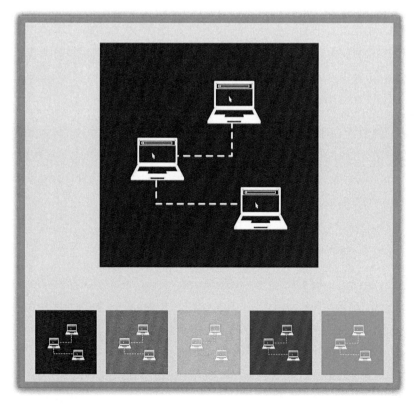

The only thing is, you want to make sure you're asking someone that has a similar amount of followers as you — otherwise, they won't get any benefit from it, and they'll either ignore you or decline.

Hold Giveaways/Contests

Start a contest that requires people to visit your blog. Sure, you're forcing their hand, but people like to win stuff, or even try to win stuff, so take advantage of the free traffic.

Use Keywords

Always use keywords in your blog. How do you know which keywords to use? Well, think about what you'd search for if you were on the Web. Let's say you want to find out some tips on how to… find keywords! You'd probably search one of the following phrases: "choosing great keywords," "how to choose keywords," "the best keywords," or "how to choose the best keywords."

When you're filling up your blog with keywords, make sure you're always thinking from a reader's perspective. What are they going to type in the search engine when they're looking for your post?

Beyond this advice, there are also online programs that help you choose keywords. These include **https://moz.com, www.spyfu. com**, and **https://landing.semrush.com**. If you get a chance, take a look at these sites and the free trials. SpyFu actually lets you type in a competitor's site to see what keywords they're using to be successful. It can be eye-opening to see the kinds of things that people are typing in, and it can help you to cater to that content.

Post to Social Media

If you have a Facebook page, link to your blog post. The same goes for every other social media application out there — start promoting yourself everywhere. If there's a chance that you'll get one new person to see your post (or even to retweet it), why not take it?

Also, make sure you're following people that are in your niche. If you write a finance blog, make sure you follow other people that write or know a lot about finance. They'll be less bothered by your constant promotions — they may even leave you the best comments!

☞ *Pro Tip:*

To boost your ability to promote yourself, create a Pinterest board for you to pin all of your posts to.

Be Patient

Blugh, we know. But, really, the best advice of all is to simply have patience. As with everything, there is no magic solution to promote your blog. It's done over time, one blog post at a time. Use the solutions and recommendations provided where possible, and over time, you will see results. It takes time, often months, to build visibility in search engines, as well as realizing the increased traffic in your promotional campaigns.

FROM THE EXPERTS: PRIYA SHAH

Find her at: www.priyashah.com, www.marketingslave.com, and www.soulkadee.com.

With the growing interest in blogging as a means of online promotion and branding, a lot of marketers are starting blogs to promote their opinions, products, books and services. But a blog is like a website. "Write and they will come" isn't exactly a magic formula to bring in traffic by the boatload.

If you need to promote your website in order to build traffic to it, you need to promote your blog as well.

Here are some ways you can become a well-read and influential blogger.

1. Write Posts That People Will Want To Read

This should be common sense, but many marketers tend to forget that their readers are real people and that you need to use the principles of online copywriting to make your headlines and copy interesting to your readers.

If you write posts that people enjoy reading, they will reward you by returning to your blog regularly. Make your posts conversational, pithy, and topical. Keep them short and stick to one topic per post. Write often and regularly so that both readers and search engines visit your blog more often.

2. Optimize Your Posts for Search Engines

I cover this topic in detail in my article on "Search Engine Optimization For Blogs" (**www.blog-maniac.com/blog-seo.htm**).

Here are the most important rules to follow to get your posts listed for keywords of your choice.

- Make sure your blog URL contains the primary keyword you want to optimize for

- Use your primary keywords in the title of your post

- Use your secondary keywords in the body of your post

- Use your keywords in the anchor text of links in the body of your posts

3. Submit Your Blog and RSS Feed To Directories

If you publish a blog, you should submit your blog and RSS feed to big directories like Yahoo and Dmoz, as well as the numerous blog directories and search engines.

Here is the best list I've found of places to submit your feed or blog, compiled by Luigi Canali De Rossi, who writes under the pseudonym Robin Good.

- Best blog directory and RSS submission sites: **www.masternew media.org/rss/top55**

- Another list of sites to submit your blog: **www.rss-specifications. com/rss-submission.htm**

4. Ping The Blog Services

There are a number of services designed specifically for tracking and connecting blogs. By sending a small ping to each service, you let them know you've updated your blog so they can come check you out.

Bookmark the Ping-O-Matic ping results page so that you can visit it and quickly ping a number of services with a single click (**http://pingo matic.com**).

5. Build Links To Your Blog

I recommend the methods here as the best ways to get links pointing to your blog:

- Trackback to other blogs in your posts

- Post legitimate comments on other blogs with related topics

- Offer to exchange links with other similarly themed blogs

6. Edit Your Blog Posts Into Articles

One of the best methods for promoting your website is to write articles and submit them to article directories.

The suggestion for extending this to edit your blog posts into articles and submit them to directories came from the coach at "Explode Blog Traffic" who also has other noteworthy suggestions at his blog here: **http://bloghit.blogspot.com/2004/11/how-to-explode-blog-traffic.html**.

You'll find an extensive list of article directories here: **http://www.article writingtips.com/submit-articles.htm**.

7. Create Buzz About Your Blog

Creating a buzz about your blog posts and topic in the local and online media will give your marketing a viral component.

- Create a controversy around your blog or its topic.

- Distribute bumper stickers or other merchandise with your blog's URL and tagline.

- Write a press release about something newsworthy and tie it in with your blog topic.

8. Capture Subscribers By Email

It may seem strange for a blogger to send out updates by email, but email is still the #1 choice of most people who want to receive news and information.

Using a free service like Bloglet to manage your subscriptions is easy, and it allows your subscribers to manage all their subscriptions from one interface (**www.bloglet.com**).

However, if you want more control over your list and don't mind mailing out the updates yourself, you can use an autoresponder system to capture and follow-up with subscribers.

RSS responder is a new script that allows you to keep in touch and follow-up with your subscribers without the hassle of email. Find it and more RSS tools here: **www.rssnewssite.com**.

These tips should give you a good start to building your blog traffic.

Priya (pronounced 'pree-yaa') Florence Shah lives in a suburb of India's financial capital, Mumbai. She is an Internet publisher, marketer, entrepreneur, and full-time mom.

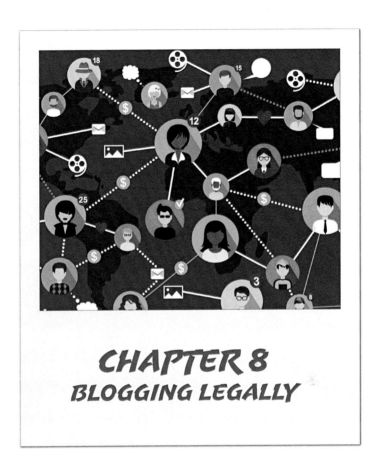

CHAPTER 8
BLOGGING LEGALLY

W hile the legal stuff might not be the most exciting thing to read about, it's important that you're familiar with it so that you don't end up in cloudy waters. There are laws about what you can and can't do on the Internet — specifically, the Communications Decency Act. The purpose of this law is basically to make sure everything is fair and appropriate.

Can Bloggers Publish Whatever They Want?

Absolutely, positively no! The best advice is to keep your blogs factual, professional, courteous, and relevant. There is no reason a blog for a corporation, organization, or worthy cause should be involved in slanderous or libelous blog postings in the first place.

> ☞ *Fast Fact:*
>
> Hal Turner, a New Jersey blogger, faces up to 10 years in prison for commenting that three Chicago judges "deserve to be killed."

There have been recent court cases in which bloggers have lost large settlements for what they have posted online, including an $11.3 million lawsuit in Florida. This appears to be a growing trend, as various bloggers are being taken to court for what they have posted.

Remember that freedom of speech is a right of every American and is one of the pillars of democracy. This entire chapter on the legalities of blogging is based entirely on United States of America law. For legal guidance on blogging in other countries, you need to contact your local legislature or communications commission.

How Am I Protected as a Blogger?

As a blogger, it is important that you understand and recognize the fact that you may be held responsible for what you say. Section 230 of the Communications Decency Act provides you with protection for "user-generated" content that may be published on your blog (there are some exceptions that we will discuss). So, if Section 230 affords you protection, why are people paying millions of dollars in libel and slander lawsuits?

The reason is that you are responsible for what you post as a blogger; however, the law, which was designed to promote free speech, protects you (as an ISP, Webmaster, administrator, etc.) from the content that "other" bloggers may post on your blog. It will provide you protection for the content published by others that may be considered slander, defamation, or libel, but it does not provide any protection for federal crimes or intellectual property violations.

This means that you can be held liable if any of these types of activities take place on your blog. So, if someone who posts on a blog may be held liable, how do you (or law enforcement) know who these individuals really are since they hide behind an online account? Recent court cases have required blog administrators and blog hosting companies to turn over identifying information pursuant to legal cases.

How Do I Avoid Legal Problems?

Include a disclaimer on your blog related to privacy, and monitor for criminal behavior and intellectual rights infringements. If you keep your blog on topic, this should never be an issue for you. Clearly indicate that you will release any privacy information (user names, real names, e-mail addresses, contact, or personal information) to law enforcement authorities pursuant to a criminal investigation.

Do not allow copyright material to be published on your blog. Do not allow criminal conduct, comments, discussions, or anything related on your blogs. Remove this type of content immediately.

Keep in mind that the law surrounding the Internet and online communications is changing all the time, and, as more blog-related cases make it through United States courts, these decisions may ultimately affect the law or the interpretation of the law. Be attentive to the ever-changing landscape of legal issues related to blogging.

**5 Most Common Mistakes that
Lead to Lawsuits (Jain 2015)**

1. **Defamation:** damaging someone's reputation

2. **Copyright Infringement:** using copyrighted
   content without permission

3. **Tortious Interference:** provoking someone to
   break a contract

4. **Right of Publicity:** using someone else's name
   on the Internet without their permission

5. **Product Disparagement:** false statements
   about a product that affect its success in the
   marketplace

Blogging Legal Review

The real problem you will have with blog spam is comments that
are posted on your blog. Most blog software applications have
built-in spam filters; make sure these are turned on. You can also
turn on features such as "approval" before a comment can actually be posted to your blog. You can also use spam blacklists to
blacklist specific words and phrases from appearing on your blog.

*Journalism Shield Laws and the
Free Flow of Information Act*

Are bloggers journalists, and are they protected from revealing
sources just as similar laws protect journalists? Even though
bloggers are often journalists by profession, the laws protecting
bloggers as journalists are a very grey area.

A "shield law" provides a news reporter or journalist with the right to refuse to testify about information and/or sources of information obtained during the course of research, confidential informants, protected sources in the process of investigating, and collecting, gathering, or disseminating news information. Currently, there is no federal shield law, and the rules vary from state to state.

The shield law is designed to protect journalists, so a blogger must be able to substantiate that they meet the definition of a journalist, which has proven to be very difficult without education, training, and credentials. The bottom line is if you don't work for a newsgathering organization or company, you probably aren't protected. But, there is hope with the Free Flow of Information Act, which may afford the same protection to bloggers as it does journalists.

You can read the Act at **www.congress.gov/bill/113th-congress/ senate-bill/987**.

Privacy data for your readers and subscribers

You can't have full control over the posting of information on your blog at all times. Likewise, you can only take so much action to prevent criminal activities or those involving slanderous or libelous blog postings by others.

You have to include a disclaimer on your blog related to privacy, monitoring for criminal behavior, and intellectual rights infringements. Keep your blog on topic, and this should never been an issue for you. An example of a good privacy policy can be viewed at **www.bigfatblog.com/about/privacy**.

Deleting content from your blog

This one will drive you crazy. You own your website and your blog. However, you do not necessarily own the content. If you allow others to post comments and add content or reviews, you don't own it.

This is considered an original work, and it's protected under copyright laws as the property of the author. The simple solution for this goes back to your terms of service that users must agree to when posting on your website or blog. They must agree that they surrender rights to anything published on your website or blog and that you have the right to modify or delete content as you see appropriate.

Having this agreement in your terms of service protects you. Without this, you may tread into dangerous waters by modifying posts without permission of the author (or owner). If your blog is fairly small, you may not have any issues, but if your blog gains traction and more and more people start to see it, you're more likely to get into legal trouble. People are crazy — we know.

Monitoring your blog for criminal activity

You must monitor your blogs for criminal activity in accordance with the Communications Decency Act. You may be protected under Section 230 for libelous or slanderous comments; however, you are not protected from criminal activity or intellectual property violations.

Intellectual property violations may be things such as distributing copyright music or DVDs. If you allow criminal activity on your website or your blog, you are subject to prosecution. Bottom line: Don't allow it, and delete it when and if it is posted on your blog.

Using images

Unless you own an image or it is royalty-free, you shouldn't post it. A common practice is to "grab" images from other Web pages. Copyright infringement occurs whenever copyrighted material is transferred to or from a website without authorization from the copyright owner; this applies to content and images.

Transferring information to and from a website can be done in several ways. You can take information from a website by copying or downloading it. Material can be uploaded from your computer to a Web server, or you can use an inline link to "pull" the image into your blog by calling that image URL but not physically pulling the image file onto your blog. As part of your terms of service, include that you retain the right to modify content to remove linking or copyright images.

This chapter merely scratches the surface of the foggy and ever-changing legalities surrounding blogging. It can be a hassle to understand, but as long as you know the basics (and use common sense), you should be fine.

☞ *Fun Fact:*

A Google search now yields almost 20 million results for "sued over a negative review."

FROM THE EXPERTS: PRIYA SHAH

Technorati reports that 30,000 to 40,000 new blogs are being created each day.

According to David Sifry, part of the growth of new blogs created each day is due to an increase in spam blogs.

What are spam blogs? They are fake blogs that are created by robots in order to foster link farms, attempted search engine optimization, or drive traffic through to advertising or affiliate sites. They contain robot-generated posts made up of random words, with the title linking back to the blogger's own pages.

Many bloggers see them as a way of getting their pages indexed quickly by Google and other search engines. Sifry estimates that about 20 percent of the aggregate pings Technorati receives are from spam blogs. Most of this fake blog spam comes from hosted services or from specific IP addresses.

Those in the SEO world are well aware of this. There are even services like Blogburner that encourage creation of spammy blogs and spam-pinging to get your sites indexed quickly. As a blogging evangelist, I wholeheartedly recommend blogging as an SEO tactic. But I also emphasize that you should use your blog for more than just SEO.

At the Spam Squashing Summit, blog services decided to collaborate to report and combat blog-spamming. Technorati currently claims to catch about 90 percent of spam and remove it from the index. They also notify the blog-hosting operators. But, I believe that they are fighting a losing battle. As I write this, there are software and robots being created that will create spam-blogs more efficiently and in ways that will be harder to detect.

The SEO "black hats" are always far ahead of the technology and safeguards that these services can put in place. Take down a few spam-blogs and hundreds more will arise. Blogging evangelist and PR guru, Steve Rubel, sums up this dilemma rather well on his Micropersuasion blog, www.micropersuasion.com. He believes that it is human nature for people to exploit new technologies, and that it's really up to the search engines to help put a stop to these by undercutting the economics of blogspam, much like they did with no follow and comment spam.

But the trade-off is that such a move would also reduce any impact that blogs have on search results. Fact: The more you abuse a technology, the less effective it becomes.

Spam blogging will force search engines like Google to change their ranking algorithms and eventually assign less value to links from blogs. Unless they put in safeguards to prevent robots from taking over, it is safe to assume that blogging will become less effective as an SEO tactic over time. Of course, the spammers will then just have to find new avenues and means to spam the engines.

But why ruin a good thing in the first place? Blogs are much more than just tools for search engine optimization. A blog can be a great tool for personal branding and building relationships with your website visitors and customers.

Instead of using blogs for spam, focus on building content-rich sites and getting high-value links to them. Don't restrict yourself to just the SEO benefits of blogging.

Appreciate the value that blogs can add to your marketing and public relations strategy and use them the way they were meant to be used.

Priya (pronounced 'pree-yaa') Florence Shah lives in a suburb of India's financial capital, Mumbai. She is an Internet publisher, marketer, entrepreneur, and full-time mom.

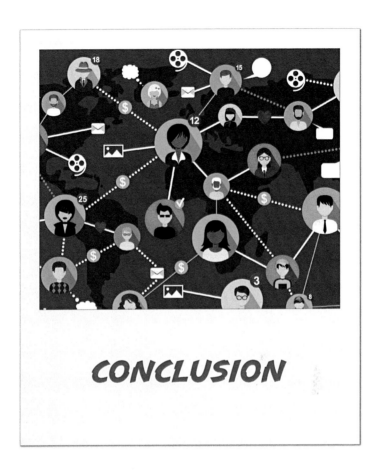

CONCLUSION

Do you feel like a blogging master? You should! You've finally reached the end, and you have everything you need to start up and maintain a successful blog.

If you use the tips we gave you in this book, you'll hopefully find success, but if you take anything away from this guide, let it be that passion is the most important part of blogging. If you aren't passionate about your topic, you won't excite anyone.

It's only appropriate to turn to the most popular blog of all time — The Huffington Post — to realize how important passion is. Writer Dave Kerpen explains (2014):

> " Passion is the energy that keeps us going, that keeps us filled with meaning, and happiness, and excitement, and anticipation. Passion is a powerful force in accomplishing anything you set your mind to. "

As if his own personal quote wasn't good enough, he went on to give 15 passionate quotes about passion. Here's my favorite:

> " I have no special talents. I am only passionately curious. " — Albert Einstein

If you're curious about something, start blogging about it. Do some research and see what you come up with. Even blogging about research is interesting — if you can take a lot of different sources and put them together, you've made it way easier for someone else to get all that information. They'll keep coming back to you if you make their life easier.

Just remember that if you have drive and motivation (and you love what you're doing), success will follow. It's inevitable.

So, go forth and start blogging.

Or something like that.

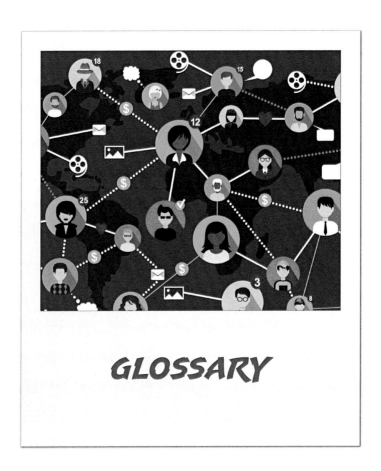

GLOSSARY

Ad

For Web advertising, an ad is almost always a banner, a graphic image, or set of animated images (in a file called an animated GIF) of a designated pixel size and byte size limit.

Ad impression

An ad impression, or ad view, occurs when a user pulls up a Web page through a browser and sees an ad that is served on that page.

Banner

A banner is an advertisement in the form of a graphic image that typically runs across a Web page or is positioned in a margin or other space reserved for ads. Banner ads are usually Graphics Interchange Format (GIF) images. Most ads are animated GIFs since animation has been shown to attract a larger percentage of user clicks. The most common larger banner ad is 468 pixels wide by 60 pixels high. Smaller sizes include 125 by 125 and 120 by 90 pixels. These and other banner sizes have been established as standard sizes by the Internet Advertising Bureau.

Aggregator

Aggregates many RSS feeds on behalf of many RSS subscribers.

Archives

A collection of all your posts on one page.

Atom

Atom is a machine-readable XML-based Web syndication format that allows users to subscribe to blogs and other Web content subject to frequent change.

Blacklist

Lists of URLs identified as spam URLs and therefore eliminated from comments and trackbacks on a blog.

Blog

Short form for Weblog. A blog is a public website with posts or entries ordered, most often, with the most recent first. Blogs generally represent the personality of the author or reflect the purpose of the website that hosts the blog. It also means to maintain a blog by posting text, links, images, or other content using blogging software.

Blog feed

The XML-based file into which blog hosting software embeds a machine-readable version of a blog to allow it to be syndicated for distribution, often through RSS and Atom.

Blog site
The location of a blog online.

Blogger
A person who creates and posts to a blog.

Blogger.com
A popular and free blog hosting website.

Blogging
The act of posting on blogs.

Blogosphere
The Internet blogging community; the collective content of all blogs worldwide.

Blogroll
A list of blogs, usually placed in the sidebar of a blog, that reads as a list of recommendations by the blogger of other blogs.

Blogspot
Hosting service for blogs operated by **Blogger.com**.

Categories
A collection of topic specific posts.

Commenter
Someone who leaves a comment on a blog.

Comment Spam
Spam posted in the comment section of blogs.

Dashboard
When you login to your blogging account, this is the first screen with all controls, tools, and functions.

Del.icio.us
The social bookmarking site where users can collectively tag favorite links.

Domain
Registered domain name.

Expression Engine
A blog publishing software package.

Feeds
RSS/XML documents containing headlines and descriptions used for Web syndication.

Keyword
A word or phrase that a user types into a search

engine when looking for specific information.

Meta tags
Hidden HTML directions for Web browsers or search engines. They include important information such as the title of each page, relevant keywords describing site content, and the description of the site that shows up when a search engine returns a search.

Open Source
A program whose source code is made available for use or modification by other developers.

Permalink
The unique URL of a single post on a blog, used when anyone wants to link specifically to a post rather than to the most recently updated page of a blog.

Ping
Used to notify other blog tracking tools of updates, changes, and trackbacks.

Plugins
Small files that add improved functionality and new features.

Post
A single unit of content on a blog, usually consisting of at least a title and text. A blog is made up of a collection of posts.

RSS
Really Simple Syndication. A method of describing news or other Web content that is available for "feeding" (distribution or syndication) from an online publisher to Web users.

RSS aggregator
Software or service that automatically checks a series of RSS feeds for new items on an ongoing basis, making it possible to keep track of changes to multiple websites in real time through one application.

RSS feed
The file that contains the latest updates to an RSS-equipped page.

RSS Reader
An application that reads many RSS feeds on behalf of one or more RSS subscriber.

Reciprocal Link
When one blogger exchanges links on its blogroll with another blogger's blogroll.

Search engine optimization (SEO)
Making a website or blog more friendly to search engines, resulting in a higher page rank.

Sidebar
One or more columns generally found on the side of most blogs.

Syndication
The distribution of a news article through an RSS or Atom feed.

Tag
Used in blogs to identify the type or types of content that makes up a particular post.

Template
The blog presentation design.

Thread
A series of remarks posted by people on a blog.

Trackback
A protocol that allows a blogger to link to posts, often on other blogs, that relate to a selected subject. Blogging software that supports trackback includes a "TrackBack URL" with each post that displays other blogs that have linked to it.

Trackback ping
A ping that signals a blog's server that a post on that blog has been commented upon.

Weblog
Longer, alternative form of blog. An online diary listing thoughts on a specific topic, often in reverse chronological order.

XML
EXtensible Markup Language; a general-purpose markup language for syndication formats used on blogs.

BIBLIOGRAPHY

Conner, Cheryl. "Battle Of The Brands: Companies With The Best Grammar Win." *Forbes*. Forbes Magazine, 17 Aug. 2013. Web. 03 May 2016.

Darling, Annika. "The 10 Top Earning Bloggers In The World." The Richest. *The Richest*, 12 Feb. 2014. Web. 03 May 2016.

Flanders, Vincent. "The 12 Worst Over-The-Top Websites of 2014." *Web Pages That Suck*. Web Pages That Suck, 2014. Web. 03 May 2016.

Hare, Kristen. "Gallery of Good Ledes, Recommendation Edition." *Poynter*. Poynter, 18 Apr. 2014. Web. 02 May 2016.

Irani, Mahafreed. "Meet the New Teen CEOs." *The Economic Times*. Bennett, Coleman & Co., 7 Nov. 2009. Web. 03 May 2016.

Jain, Shilpi. "5 Common Mistakes Leading to Lawsuits against Bloggers." *QuickGulp*. QuickGulp, 06 Jan. 2015. Web. 03 May 2016.

Jatain, Vishveshwar. "10 Blogging Statistics You Probably Didn't Know But Should." *AdPushup*. AdPushup, 04 May 2015. Web.
03 May 2016.

Kerpen, Dave. "Why Passion Matters, According To 15 Of The World's Most Inspiring People." *The Huffington Post*. TheHuffingtonPost.com, 2 Apr. 2014. Web. 03 May 2016.

Mohan, Mahesh. "How Much Traffic Do You Need To Make $100,000 With AdSense." *Minterest*. Minterest, 03 Jan. 2016. Web. 03 May 2016.

Olenski, Steve. "4 Myths About Affiliate Marketing You Need To Know." *Forbes*. Forbes Magazine, 8 July 2014. Web. 04 May 2016.

Salter, Jessica. "Meet the Children Blogging about Their World." *The Telegraph*. Telegraph Media Group, 15 Mar. 2013. Web. 03 May 2016.

Shoaf, Jeremiah. "The 10 Most Popular Web Fonts of 2015." *Typewolf.* Typewolf, 12 Jan. 2016. Web. 03 May 2016.

Simone, Seleah. "Teen Dream: The Top Bloggers Under 18." *Guest of a Guest.* Guest of a Guest Inc., 12 Jan. 2012. Web. 03 May 2016.

Staff. "Business of Beauty: Zoella, A Star from Across the Pond." *VideoInk.* Video Ink, 12 July 2013. Web. 2 May 2016.

Tweedy, Spencer. "Tweedy Tour 2014." *Medium.* Medium, 09 Dec. 2014. Web. 03 May 2016.

University of Pennsylvania. "'Hairy' Potter and the Tale of a Mumbai Teen Blogger." *Entrepreneurship & Leaders.* The Wharton School, University of Pennsylvania, 1 Mar. 2013. Web. 3 May 2016.

Widdicombe, Lizzie. "Tavi Says." *The New Yorker.* N.p., 13 Sept. 2010. Web. 02 May 2016.

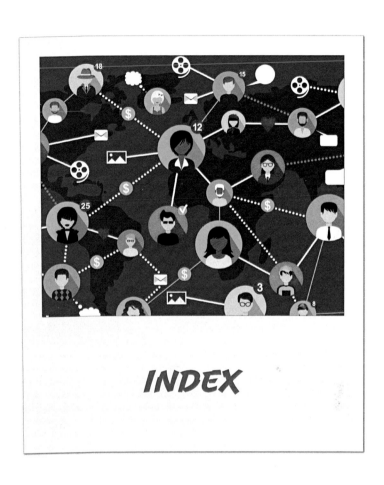

INDEX

AUTHOR BIO

Rebekah Sack is a young adult nonfiction author. Her books cover topics such as bullying, interviewing, nutrition, confidence, and writing. She also manages Atlantic Publishing's young adult blog (**https://atlanticteen.wordpress.com**) which features posts about writing, reading, publishing, and general life tips. A summa cum laude graduate of Illinois State University, she now works for Atlantic Publishing as the in-house editor.